MW01285079

EMBRACING YOUR MONEY POWER

A WOMAN'S GUIDE TO FINANCIAL FREEDOM

MONIQUE FREDERICK

Copyright © 2024 Monique Frederick. All rights reserved.

No part of this book may be reproduced or transmitted in any form or by any means without written permission of the publisher, except in the case of brief quotations embedded in critical articles and reviews.

Statements made and opinions expressed in this publication are those of the author and do not necessarily reflect the views of the publisher or indicate an endorsement by the publisher.

DEDICATION

This book is dedicated to my late father, Paul Kappel. He lived a life illustrating that with grit, dedication, and commitment; anything was achievable. Throughout my childhood, he always instilled in me the importance of learning. He always advocated that knowledge was the key to setting yourself up for success. My dad had an entire library of books covering various subjects, including business & finance. He did not have a university degree; he was self-taught, and his hundreds and hundreds of books were proof of that.

Although my dad was instrumental in introducing me to the world of investments and ensuring that I always strived to be exceptional in any endeavor, I am genuinely grateful for the unwavering support from my mom throughout my life. Without her involvement in chauffeuring my sister and me up and down to after-school activities, offering to help us study for exams, taking us to extra exam prep classes at night or on weekends, and making sure our future would be financially better than her childhood, I would not be the same person I am today.

This book is also dedicated to the friends and wonderful people who have encouraged me to write this book. I have always enjoyed educating and encouraging others, whether it's through one-on-one conversations or speaking engagements, but it's the recommendations and requests I have received to share the message with others who would benefit from it that led me to write this book.

Finally, I would like to thank the transformational speaker and best-selling author Lisa Nichols for inspiring me to put pen to paper and share my insights with the universe so it may benefit the woman or man who's been waiting for the right person with the right message at the right time.

Table of Contents

INTRODUCTION

With over two decades of experience in the investment industry guiding, advising, and assisting individuals and institutions in achieving their financial goals, I have realized that simplifying the world of investments and inspiring others is a true passion of mine.

As the first chartered financial analyst in my family and a female in a predominantly male field, leading a team of qualified investment professionals is something that I have much to be proud of.

As a speaker and a former director of various professional associations as well as my involvement in the performing arts, I'm considered by many to be an inspiration to girls and young women. I am confident in my abilities with a clear strategy of what I want to achieve and unfazed by being a woman in a man's world.

However, I did not start out that way

It was at the tender age of twelve when my young and highly formative mind witnessed how imperfect the world we live in is. My best friend at the time was one of the most beautiful girls in my middle school, and from the outside in, I'm sure everyone thought she had a perfect life. I used to spend a lot of time at her house, and it was always a home filled with laughter and chatter as family and friends were always stopping by.

On this particular day, the atmosphere was unlike any other. Her mom was walking around the house dressed in an oversized T-shirt, mumbling and bitter at the same time. I learned that day that my best friend's mom and dad were getting a divorce.

I remember, as a young girl, trying to wrap my mind around her feelings. She had once been a radiant bride, eyes filled with the dream of a lifetime of love and partnership. Yet, as the chapters of her life unfolded, she was confronted with realities that diverged from those dreams. How many times did she look in the mirror, thinking of all she had given, the dreams she set aside? Maybe for her children, maybe for love? Could she have chased her own career, or did she wholeheartedly choose the nurturing heartbeat of her home? In giving so much, did she perhaps forget to give to herself? Each decision becomes a story, teaching us that life's journey is filled with unexpected turns and, most importantly, lessons of resilience.

Although I did not know every little detail, this painful event had a tremendous impact on me. How could I ensure that my future did not end up like that? Although they were not my parents getting a divorce, the sorrow and the bitterness urged me to promise myself to always be ready and able to take care of myself.

That meant I had to learn to take care of myself. I had to learn to provide for myself. It meant I could stand up for myself against boys. If I didn't know how to do something, I would research it. It meant I would not rely on someone else to provide for me. I wanted to control my destiny as much as possible. Ultimately, that meant becoming financially independent.

Although I set my goal of financial independence at a very young age, that journey certainly wasn't without its challenges along the way. I knew that to achieve financial independence, I needed a good career, and for a good career, I needed a good education as well as the necessary academic accolades. So that's where my focus was: my education and my grades. I should mention that it wasn't just my focus; it was my dad's primary focus as well. Everything was going according to plan- I was even scheduled to compete in the National Physics Olympiad while in high school, a competition for which I had been preparing for many weeks. However, the day before the competition, my dad sat me down to convey the most shocking, dreadful, and agonizing news a child could hear.

"I have cancer," he said in a matter-of-fact way.

"What?" I responded, hoping I had not heard him correctly.

Once he reconfirmed, I immediately went into problem-solving mode, bombarding my dad with numerous questions and trying to give him advice. *Have you tried so and so therapy? Maybe you need to go to church.* The seriousness and the heft of the situation had not really set in until the next morning when I entered the room to sit the exam for the National Physics Olympiad. The winners would represent the country at the International Physics Olympiad. Once the exam proctor gave all of us the go-ahead to get started, I read the first question but I felt like I was staring into the abyss. Nothing made sense. The only thing I could think of was my dad's cancer diagnosis. All the studying, extra university-level classes, my reputation as an A+ student, and the high expectations from my teachers came crashing down that Saturday morning. I could not think clearly, could not concentrate, and was not able to answer any question, an experience that was completely foreign to me.

I know that everyone reading this book has had one or several experiences where the one thing you have been working on so diligently or the goal you were making great progress toward suddenly comes crashing down. It could be a death in the family, a life-threatening illness, a natural disaster, a divorce, a betrayal, a family member who desperately needs your help, or a bad financial decision you happened to have entered into. We have all been there at some point in our lives. For some of us, it may have been while growing up or while pursuing a tertiary education, while for others it may have been while starting a family or much later in life.

My family structure, albeit pleasant, wasn't perfect, and throughout my university years as well as throughout my career as an investment professional, I have come across so many situations where women are left completely financially deprived. This can be due to a failed marriage, the untimely death of a spouse, or a major medical event in the family. There are still so many women, even in this day and age, who are leaving the financial decisions to their spouse or partner. There are still so many women whose parents never really discussed money and investing with them growing up.

Fortunately, there are a growing number of women who are very much interested in being financially independent, and some of them have even achieved success in their careers but haven't made the time to focus on their personal well-being and, consequently, their personal financial planning. I know quite a few professional women, myself included, who fit into this category. We're the group who have set out to obtain financial independence early on by focusing on career growth: the ambitious women who have managed to climb the corporate ladder and are now accountants, lawyers, doctors, and small business owners. Our achievements are the result of hard work, dedication, and a tremendous focus on client or patient needs. While these attributes have made us successful in having the skills and experience to always land a job and therefore being able to provide for ourselves when needed, some of us have also neglected our own wellness in the process. That includes long-term financial wellness and financial planning.

Friends, colleagues, acquaintances, and family have asked for guidance throughout the years, but I have also come to find out some women are too afraid to ask. Just based on demographics, more women are becoming responsible for their household finances. Based on the feedback and requests from the many amazing women I have met and based on my experiences both professionally and personally, I have been inspired to assist women in uncovering their inherent strengths to embark on their financial independence journey. I'm convinced that in the same way that women have been able to overcome all kinds of challenges, including completely unfamiliar ones, they are also capable of mastering their own financial independence.

This book is meant to dispel the myths about investing while simultaneously arming you with confidence and knowledge to embark on the journey toward financial freedom, regardless of where you are starting from.

I hope that along with reading this book, you will also put the knowledge you learn into practice. It's the only way to truly achieve financial freedom and success. While I have tried to include all of the tips and investing wisdom I've learned in my personal and professional life, your financial position is unique. Don't be afraid to try something new on your journey toward mastering what you need to be financially independent in your life.

———————

"The journey of a thousand miles begins with a single step."

Lao Tzu

CHAPTER 1

Don't Believe the Lie

There was a period in time growing up when I felt that I did not belong. I transferred to a private high school where my aunt was the physics teacher. Truth be told, she wasn't actually my aunt. She was my sister. However, if your sister is so much older than you that she could be your mother, it would be considered rude to call her by her first name. I was clearly instructed by my dad that she should be referred to as my aunt.

Given that she was my half-sister, we did not have the same mother, and her own two sons were attending the same high school as me. It certainly seemed much easier to call her Auntie. How do you explain to your classmates and friends that her two sons who are older than you are actually not your cousins but instead your nephews?

Imagine how many more looks and questions you would receive. Although I would have been ready to defend myself, the idea of being singled out or being made fun of felt like eating something exceptionally spicy followed by severe acid reflux. These are facts about my family I never discussed while growing up. As an adult, I quickly came to realize that this scenario was not as uncommon as I thought, but as a child, the thought of being the only child in the entire school with such a strange family structure was terrifying. I felt like the odd one out.

Today, on the subject of investments, many women still feel like the odd one out. This is partially due to another misconception that women cannot hold on to or keep track of their money. Has someone ever told you that women simply aren't good with math or money? Even now, the belief is still prevalent in some male-dominated circles. Did you know that in most households, women manage the budget?

Paying the monthly bills as well as grocery shopping comes to mind. The movie industry and social media have perpetuated the idea of women being overspenders. Indeed, women spend more money on shoes, apparel, and personal care in general, but men spend more on big-ticket items like TVs and cars. On the other hand, women are more inclined to shop for bargains and compare prices. These days, you don't need to drive from store to store; while you're in one store, you can immediately look up prices on your phone.

Historically, women have spent more on education and books while men have typically spent more on eating out, entertainment, and alcohol and tobacco. The image portrayed by just a few celebrities, influencers, and female movie characters does not accurately reflect the overall female population. The message that women can't manage their money even extends to advertising. While men have several media outlets devoted to providing information on investing, it's almost impossible to find a publication geared toward female investors. Once again, women can get the feeling they don't belong.

Fathers, especially in certain cultures, are more likely to discuss financial concepts with their sons, leaving their daughters out of the conversation. Unfortunately, most women are still earning less money than their male counterparts. These realities reinforce the misconception that women don't belong in the investment world.

A lie (myth) I often hear is that women are averse to risk. Almost everyone prefers to avoid risks unless you are a thrill seeker. Investing can be a rollercoaster ride of thrills and disappointments, but it doesn't mean women aren't willing to step out of their comfort zone. Most women take some risk throughout their lives from marriage to childbirth and beyond. There are other factors at play here.

Women with investment portfolios tend to hold on to their stocks longer. They trade less frequently and are more focused on the long-term goal. Avoiding knee-jerk reactions to market movements has proven to be cost-saving for women, resulting in better long-term performance. Additionally, women tend to have more balanced portfolios, resulting in less volatility overall. All these actions point to a more conservative investment approach, not an unwillingness to participate. That approach is not surprising because we know in the back of our minds that any financial decisions we make today will impact our family in the future.

Throughout my many years in the industry, I have noticed that women are undoubtedly interested in investment conversations. Still, they want to speak with someone they can relate to. Someone who won't make them feel like they don't belong at the table. Someone who will understand what's important to them beyond just the numbers. Someone who understands their financial goals as well as their life challenges.

However, when they look for an investment company online, what do they see?

In most instances, when looking at the company photo, you can count the number of women in the picture on one hand. Many women I have had the pleasure of speaking with are uncomfortable entrusting their finances to a company or portfolio manager who does not understand the concerns many women have about investing their money. Talk about not feeling welcome when you are the only female in the room.

We have all been in situations where we felt we did not belong. Can you imagine your musically inclined friends dragging you to an impromptu performance, but you have never touched a musical instrument before? Or a friend invites you along to a gathering of physics Ph.D. candidates, and you don't understand anything they're talking about? Maybe it goes beyond a feeling of technical inferiority. You walk into a room and everyone is talking about their private jets, and you're worried about buying a new economy car.

What comes to mind when you hear the words stocks, mutual funds, ETFs, or IPOs? Is it confusing and overwhelming? Maybe it all seems like a foreign language you may have been forced to study in high school and immediately dropped as soon as you had the chance. On the other hand, the images conjured up in your head may be ones of billionaires or older Caucasian men dressed in expensive suits driving luxury cars. Historically, the media and movies have portrayed the wealthy as only two categories: celebrities or CEOs running large technology firms or financial institutions.

Over a decade ago, if you had watched the financial news on television, you would have only seen one type of demographic represented. So, it's not surprising that many people I have come across who are not in the financial services industry never really felt that investing was something for them. For a long time, and to some extent still today, there has been the belief that you must be wealthy before you can or should start investing. The adage "You need money to make money" comes to mind. Although you need to put in money to make more money, in this day and age, it certainly isn't true that you need a lot of money to get started.

If the many investment acronyms are confusing, you are not alone. Even if you were among the lucky ones and your high school provided an introductory finance class, those classes did not really touch on investing. Most likely, your teacher spent much of the class discussing traditional bank accounts like checking and savings. Don't feel like you need a degree to understand all the investment terms that exist. Let me let you in on a little secret; your brother, uncle, or male co-worker do not understand all of the investment terms either. While you don't need a degree to start investing, it does help to have a basic understanding of the common terms, and throughout this book, I will introduce them to you. The goal is to make you feel comfortable investing your money so you can secure your financial freedom.

Having a basic understanding of terms associated with investing will help you feel like you belong. However, there are a lot of terms associated with investing beyond ETFs, mutual funds, etc. Understanding the key terms will make it a little easier for you to reach your financial goals. After all, if you don't know the lingo, it's difficult to carry on a conversation with your broker or other type of financial adviser. Even online trading platforms can seem daunting when you aren't sure how asset allocation, compound interest, and other terms apply to your investments.

I regularly talk about assets. The term applies to anything with economic value. Cash, bonds, and stocks are examples of assets. If you own your home, it's an asset. In the simplest terms, an asset is anything someone is willing to purchase. It can even include your grandmother's antique China set, as long as you have interested buyers. The value of your assets can also fluctuate. One look at the ups and downs of the stock market is a good example.

When you add different types of assets to a single portfolio, it's known as asset allocation. Keeping all your investments in one portfolio can make it easier to track your various investments. When asset allocation is done properly, your unique financial goals are taken into consideration to ensure the largest return on your investments for a certain level of risk.

Capital gains are something I want every female investor to be familiar with. It refers to the profit you collect when a stock or other type of investment sells for a profit. Take a real estate investment. Your purchased property sells for more than the purchase price, and you recoup any money you used for renovations, repairs, and taxes. Compound interest is another term I want to touch on. It can be beneficial, or it can cost you money. The term refers to the interest earned on an account or loan. When it applies to an account, it is earned money. Interest builds up over time with some types of accounts, like savings accounts. When it is applied to loans, it is the amount of interest you end up paying back. So, if you borrow $1,000, you are paying back the initial amount plus the total compounded interest. Before taking out a loan, compare interest rates. Interest rates typically vary by lender, type of loan, and your credit score.

If you played the game of Monopoly as a child or with your children, some of the cards in the Chance and the Community Chest decks mention paying you a dividend on your stocks. A dividend is a portion of the company's profits paid to investors. You can receive dividends annually, monthly, or quarterly depending on how the investment is structured. You can track dividend amounts and payment dates easily online. Several investment sites post the calendar, along with NASDAQ, on its official site. Tracking dividends is always a good way to get an idea of what your potential earnings can be if you invest in the company.

Your return is a term you will frequently come across, and it refers to your profit or loss on an investment over a specific amount of time. If you invested $1000 in a stock and sold it a year later for $1200 while also receiving $20 in dividends during the year, your net gain would be $220 (($1200 - $1000) + $20). Your return on the stock would be 22% ($220 divided by the original cost of $1000). Like dividends, returns can also give you a good idea of how an investment is performing. For those of you who are averse to risk, it's an effective way of learning if the stock is historically safe.

Risk tolerance is different for every investor. It's the level of risk you are willing to take on an investment. It's also an essential component used to create your investment portfolio. If you prefer to take less risk and are willing to wait for the investment to pay off, your portfolio will contain lower-risk stocks, bonds, and other types of investments. The opposite is true for investors with a higher risk tolerance and who want to see a faster return. Be comfortable with your risk tolerance. It will make investing less stressful, and you may even have fun watching your investments grow.

Becoming familiar with the various terms doesn't mean you know everything there is to learn about investing. However, it can give you more confidence in making decisions on which investments are best suited to achieve your financial goals, whether you are investing with an online platform, a brokerage firm, or with the assistance of an investment advisor.

The number of online trading platforms catering to non-investment professionals has increased sharply in the past few years, making access to financial markets the easiest it has ever been.

These online trading platforms have advantages missing in most traditionally structured brokerage firms. Instead of waiting for an investment advisor to contact you periodically or for them to return your phone call, you are in complete control of your investments. In the online investing world, everyone belongs. You can buy and sell stocks in real time, including checking current prices.

Since a common concern is a lack of available funds, online trading lets you start investing as little or as much as you want. Is one of the reasons you refrain from investing due to your limited capital and because you don't want to feel embarrassed in a broker's office? Online trading platforms are a cost-effective way to start planning for your financial independence.

Are you tired of hearing that you won't understand market data? It's a common complaint I hear from friends, family, and other women. You can get access to market data at any time. You can make informed decisions about your portfolio. Even when your portfolio only consists of a couple of stocks, it's still important to track its progress. Following the current market data is also a good way to educate yourself and minimize your potential risks. Think of it as the class you should have been offered in school. One of the other ways online trading platforms are making it easier to access financial markets is the ability to track investments from almost any internet-connected device. Around-the-clock access and prompt support from customer service provide the assistance that beginners often need.

So, why do so many people still not participate in the stock market?

Financial literacy is not a subject that is included in the traditional education system. Learning about budgeting, credit cards, insurance, and investments is not a part of the curriculum taught in schools, although it's the foundation required for financial health in adulthood. Maybe you're lucky enough that your parents or family discussed money in your house growing up. Unfortunately for most people, that certainly wasn't the case. Talking about money was taboo in their house. You wouldn't dare to ask your parents how much money they were making, and if you did, they would have answered, "It's none of your business." Instead, money was only talked about in the context of scarcity.

I know many of us were told the phrase "Money doesn't grow on trees" over and over again while growing up. For many, the focus was on not having enough money and consequently trying to find ways to stretch every dollar. Our parents' generation somehow found a way to make every dollar stretch. I remember a story my late aunt told me about raising her five children as a single mother. One of her sons, like many children today, always wanted name-brand clothing. He did not want to go to school with a no-name-brand shirt from some discount clothing store. This was before the invention of social media over thirty-five years ago.

So what did she do? She was quite resourceful. She removed the label from the shirts and pants she bought him and sewed on labels from the brands he loved. She would take the handful of old name-brand items he had and re-use the labels. As a young boy, he did not know the difference. As far as he knew, he was walking around in the latest Prada jeans. In today's social media–controlled world, this act would probably backfire. Regardless, I am always amazed by the money-saving measures our mothers used to come up with.

In some households, parents did talk about the need to be frugal with money and about spending it carefully, but the subjects of saving and how to make your money work for you in the future did not come up at all. Although that's regrettable, it's not surprising because our parents were not armed with financial literacy skills either. Unless they were self-taught or happened to work in the financial sector, the likelihood of them having that knowledge to pass on was slim. Not only did saving and budgeting not come up in conversations, but the subject of money was contentious in some homes. It was the one topic some of my friends remember their parents arguing about.

The fact that no one in your family discussed investments or the fact that it seems like a foreign language to you doesn't mean it wasn't meant for you. I have met so many people whose parents instilled the values of hard work and dedication in order to achieve success, and I embody those values myself. However, hard work by itself is not enough. So many people work more than one job in order to survive. If there were more hours in a day, they would cram in a third or fourth job if possible.

On top of that, everything gets more expensive every year. The same hamburger you could buy five years ago doesn't cost the same today. Inflation is alive and well. So is shrinkflation, the art of hidden inflation. Have you noticed that the price of a box of hot chocolate packets hasn't changed, but instead, the number of packets in a box has declined? Inflation alone makes the value of the money you do have decrease over time.

Regardless of your past, your upbringing, or lack of awareness, now is the time to get started.

Depending on your current financial circumstances, you may consider the word "investment" a hallucination. If you're trying to make ends meet and you can barely keep your head above water financially, why would you even think about investments? You're probably more worried about how you'll pay the bills this month. Who has the time to think about investments in this situation? While this is understandable, the time to think about financial planning is now and not when your life is perfect. Not only is "perfect" unattainable, but perfectionism can lead to inaction and procrastination. When you were a baby, your parents did not expect you to run at one month old. You gradually moved from sitting to crawling to walking and running. When you first attempted to stand and pull yourself up, I'm sure your parents were watching you full of excitement and silently cheering you on. They would not have said, "Don't try standing up until all the conditions are right".

As a parent, you would not have instructed your little one to sit back down. You're not waiting for perfection.

There is no perfect time to start investing. No one, not even financial advisors and money managers, can perfectly time the best day to invest in the stock market. We don't have a crystal ball to give us the perfect day, hour, or minute to buy a stock. What we do know is that you have to be in it to win it. History has also shown that despite market volatility—some years you may lose money and some you make money—in the long run, you make money. The earlier you start, the better. We have a tendency to say, "I'll wait until I have a higher-paying job, and then I'll put some money aside to invest." We think that when we have more money to put aside, it will have a greater impact. Let me share a secret: a small amount invested on a regular basis starting now can actually result in a larger retirement fund rather than waiting until you have more to invest years from now.

If Jane invested $100 monthly in the stock market starting today, assuming an average annual return of 8%, she would have close to $57,000 in twenty years. Compare that to Steve, who waits until ten years from now, when he can invest $200 per month for ten years. Twenty years from now, Steve will end up with $36,000. Steve waited to invest double the amount Jane invested in half the time but ended up with less. This scenario illustrates that the earlier you start, the better. Don't wait until you think you have a lot. Start small.

The lack of knowledge and understanding is another reason often cited as to why many have stayed away from investments. We want to ensure we understand what we're committing our hard-earned money to. I feel the same way when I go to the doctor. The moment the doctor prescribes some medication and mentions a word I have never heard before, I'm Googling it. By the time I have read all the side effects of the prescribed medication, I'm inclined not to take it all.

When preparing for that milestone day of becoming a parent of twin boys, I did a tremendous amount of groundwork. My husband and I attended prenatal classes, and I read books on becoming a parent, including a book on raising twins. I did prenatal pilates classes, and I researched pediatricians before choosing one. I spent hours on Google. Some of the information was informative, some of it was worrisome, and some of it completely stressed me out. In today's world of information at our fingertips, we can quickly feel overwhelmed or talk ourselves out of doing anything.

When it comes to investing, many of us take that same approach. We want the knowledge to fully understand it before taking that first step. Yet, when we decide to hop on a plane to visit family for Thanksgiving, we don't think about our inability to fly the plane if something happens to the pilot. We just research the airline, and as long as it's a reliable airline, we don't really consider the pilot's qualifications or the security of the aircraft itself. We place our trust in the airline and expect them to get us there safely.

While it's important to be aware of what you're investing in, you don't need a Ph.D. in the subject to participate in it. Starting small and gradually while learning the basics should be sufficient to get you started. There are so many websites, as well as apps, that provide access to introductory information if you want to start out on your own. Alternatively, financial advisors can guide you as well.

Steps to Financial Freedom:

1. Search for a budgeting tool or budgeting spreadsheet online and complete your monthly expenses, income, & intended monthly savings

2. Write down your long-term financial goal (kids' college savings, retirement, down payment for a house)

"Step out of the history that is holding you back. Step into the new story you are willing to create"

Oprah Winfrey.

CHAPTER 2

It's Already in You

Would you go skydiving without a helmet? Would you go for a swim in piranha-infested waters? How about poking a bear in the woods?

There is a certain level of risk in every single thing we do. When we get in our car every day, there is a risk of a car accident, even if we have an impeccable driving record. We can't eliminate all risks, but we can mitigate them. When jumping into our car, we try to reduce the possibility of damaging our car or getting injured by ensuring we don't drink and drive, by not texting and driving, and by paying attention.

That's the same approach to take when investing. Some of us are scared of investments, and that's fully understandable. There are lots of examples in the news that would raise concerns. Whether it's a bank or investment firm going bankrupt, an uncovered investment Ponzi scheme, or your parents losing more than half of their pension during the global financial crisis, they all highlight what can go wrong. The global financial crisis was all too real for so many. We saw the impact on grandparents and parents. In some cases, our own financial well-being was severely affected. No one wants to lose their hard-earned money.

When it comes to investing, there is a risk of losing money, especially in the short term, but if you decided not to drive again because of the risk of an accident, you would not be able to get to work to earn a living, and you would have zero income. The same applies here. Instead of not participating at all, you should take steps to mitigate the risk.

First, you decide on the level of risk you're willing to take. For example, you can decide to drive a car to work, take the train, take an Uber, or cycle to work. In some cities, cycling to work is the riskiest option. Even with this knowledge, you may still decide to cycle to work because it provides specific benefits such as exercise and better health. In an attempt to reduce the risk of an accident, you decide to wear a helmet and some reflective gear as well as install a horn.

While all of us have the ability to reduce the amount of risk we're exposed to every day; mothers seem inherently good at mitigating risk. Do you remember all the protective measures you put in place when your kids were toddlers? Childproofing your home consists of locking away dangerous cleaning supplies, using outlet covers, and installing cabinet locks. But what about outside the home? Kids are always interested in doing something they see their friends doing.

I remember when my kids were invited to a six-year-old's birthday party at a skatepark. Neither my husband nor I had ever skateboarded, and neither did we intend to try it as adults. I had them dressed in all the possible protective gear: a helmet, knee pads, elbow pads, and wrist guards. As they stepped off the edge of the first skating bowl, I had my hand on my chest. I felt like I was about to jump off the edge. My lungs deflated, and I held my breath, finally inhaling again once I did not hear any screams and saw that they were still moving.

Before the party, they tried skateboarding on the road (a flat surface) and I did arrange for one lesson with an instructor, but that doesn't make you a pro. All was going well at the party as I stood at the side of the skatepark the entire time, trying to keep an eye on both of my sons. Suddenly, I heard a scream, and my heart stopped. There was a section of the park I could not see from where I was standing that wasn't accessible without either skating to it or walking or climbing through a few bowls. I got as close as I could as quickly as I could, but I still couldn't see my boys. It took what felt like a lifetime before I saw one of my sons appear and declare that his brother was hurt. When I saw my other son limping toward me, I was worried but relieved that he was able to walk. He had some scrapes, but luckily, the protective gear averted a worse outcome.

We try so hard to protect our young ones, but then they get older, and you can't protect them any longer. I have stopped counting the number of phone calls I have received from the school nurse throughout the years because of falls, cuts, ankle injuries, and head injuries. Some of them resulted in emergency visits to the hospital. I have learned throughout the years that we can't control everything. We can limit our exposure to risk by staying away from certain situations, or we can take the necessary steps to reduce the potential risks that exist when participating in certain activities or visiting certain places.

The kind of steps we're willing to take is dependent on our risk tolerance. Some of my friends love rollercoasters while others refuse to set foot on one. Some are thrill-seekers while some prefer to play it safe. Some of us don't mind being adventurous in some areas of our lives while being extremely conservative in other areas. There are reasons why we react differently, which I'll return to later in the book.

From an investment perspective, we first want to determine how much risk we can tolerate. It's not just about how much risk you're able to take but also how much you're able to handle.

When it comes to personal finance, your risk tolerance is important. It's basically how much risk you're comfortable taking with your investments, which can vary from person to person. Your age, income, financial goals, and personal preferences all play a role in determining your risk tolerance. Let's explore this concept a bit more with some real-life examples.

First up is age. Generally, younger folks have a higher risk tolerance than older folks because they have more time to recover from any losses. For example, a twenty-five-year-old investor might be more willing to invest in a high-risk stock than a sixty-year-old investor because the twenty-five-year-old has more time to bounce back from any losses.

Income is another factor to consider. Folks with higher incomes tend to have a higher risk tolerance than those with lower incomes. This is because they have more money to play around with and can afford to take on more risks. For example, someone with a high income might be more willing to invest in a high-risk stock because they have a safety net if things don't go as planned.

Your financial goals are also a big factor in determining your risk tolerance. If you have short-term goals, you should not take on too much risk with your investments. On the other hand, if you have long-term goals, you might be more open to taking on some risks. For example, if you're saving up for a down payment on a house, you might want to stick with lower-risk investments. However, if you're saving for retirement, you might be more willing to take on some risk because you have more time to recover from any losses.

Real-life examples can help illustrate the concept of risk tolerance even more. Let's say we have two people: Sarah and John. Sarah is a thirty-year-old who makes a good income and is saving for retirement. John is a fifty-year-old with a lower income saving up for a down payment on a house. Sarah has a higher risk tolerance than John because she has more time to recover from losses. She might choose to invest in high-risk stocks because she knows she has a long time horizon. However, John might stick with lower-risk investments because he needs to preserve his savings for his down payment.

Basically, the amount of risk you can take is highly dependent on your investment time horizon. How much time do you have to achieve your specific financial goal? Generally, the shorter your time horizon, the lower the level of risk you can afford to take. If you're saving for your retirement twenty years from now, you can invest more of your savings in stocks, which are considered riskier than cash and bonds. Investing in stocks will allow your money to grow and beat inflation over time. On the other hand, for shorter-term investment goals, such as school fees due two years from now, placing 100% of your savings in stocks is certainly not a good idea.

When it comes to risk tolerance, the easiest way to understand your tolerance for risk is by asking yourself this question: If I had investments and the stock market went down 5% today, would I be able to sleep tonight, or would I be up all night sweating and panicking? If you have sleepless nights, you would be better off investing conservatively with a lower allocation to stocks.

You might say, "Well, what does 5% actually mean?" Imagine you are helping your child set up a lemonade stand. Let's say that all the materials and ingredients cost $10. If the lemonade stand only earned back 50 cents, you (and your child) would be pretty disappointed, and you should be. This would represent a 95% loss on your investment in their little business! However, would you be as disappointed if you only made back $9.50? That would be a 5% loss. What if it was $5, a 50% loss?

Ten dollars isn't a lot to most adults. However, if your initial investment is $100 or $1,000, losing 50% would be like losing $50 or $500, but losing 5% is more like losing $5 or $50 respectively. Relative to your initial investment, are you okay with losing that amount?

Investments, whether directly in a business or through stocks, always require you to take some risks. It is not only important for you to know when you are going to pull your money out if your losses drop too far, but also how much faith you have in your investment to gain back its losses.

In our lemonade stand analogy, do you have faith in your child and their ability to sell more lemonade? Is there evidence that they can still sell more? If the lemonade is all gone, then selling more would require an additional investment. However, if there are still cups and lemonade available to sell, then there is still a potential upside for your investment. Do you have the time? If you only have ten minutes and no one is on the street, you might cut your losses. Yet, if you have thirty minutes or an hour to spare, giving up when they are down 5%, 50 cents short of breaking even, you may decide it is worth waiting to see if they can sell more.

Do you have similar faith and patience for your investments? Ask yourself- do I need that $95 back today? The stock market can make or lose hundreds of thousands of dollars in an hour, or it could lose a quick 5% and sit there for days on end. Yes, your risk tolerance should always be based on how much you are willing to lose. Are you going to fret when you are down $5? What if you knew that the company was solid and outside forces contributed to a bad quarter for them? This would be comparable to a quick rainstorm at your lemonade stand where you couldn't sell anything for a half-hour.

Imagine that the company you invested in had a new technology they announced but the release date got pushed back two weeks. You might not be as concerned about losing $5 today because you have a belief that the stock you have in that company is going to go up once the technology is released.

On the other hand, do you need your money today? Then definitely fret about the $5. Can you wait two weeks, and does your evidence show you have reason to believe it will go back up? That is your risk tolerance. Set your threshold for loss (the 5%), do your research, and set your timeline.

You already make investment decisions!

We all make investment decisions every single day. If you decided to attend college, you made an investment in your education and future earnings potential. When you decide to go on a trip, you're making an investment in your mental health. When you help your kids with homework and studying, you're investing in their education. When you decide not to buy a latte or go for a fancy dinner today and instead decide to put the money aside in your savings account, you make an investment decision. You opted for cash, but it's still a financial investment decision.

We make small investment decisions every day without even realizing it. These decisions may seem insignificant, but they can add up over time and have a significant impact on our financial well-being.

One of the most common small investment decisions we make is choosing where to buy our morning coffee. If we opt for a fancy coffee shop every day, we could be spending hundreds or even thousands of dollars a year on coffee alone. Instead, we could invest in a quality coffee maker and make our own coffee at home. This small change could save us a lot of money in the long run.

Another small investment decision we make is choosing what to eat for lunch. If we opt for fast food or takeout every day, we could be spending a significant amount of money on food. Instead, we could invest in a meal prep kit or cook our own meals at home. This little change could not only save us money, but also improve our health and well-being.

We also make small investment decisions when it comes to our entertainment choices. For example, choosing to go to the movies every weekend can be expensive. Instead, we could invest in a streaming service. This small change could save us a lot of money in the long run.

When it comes to transportation, we also make small investment decisions every day. Choosing to drive to work every day can be expensive due to the cost of gas and maintenance. Instead, we could invest in a bike or public transportation pass. This small change could save us money and also benefit the environment.

Even the trivial decisions we make when shopping can have a significant impact on our finances. For example, buying a generic brand instead of a name brand can save us money in the long run. We can also look for sales and discounts to save even more money.

The small investment decisions we make every day can have a significant impact on our financial well-being. By making small changes to our daily routines, we can save money and improve our overall quality of life. It's important to be mindful of these small decisions and make choices that are in our best interest.

You may be wondering why I'm comparing investing in your child's education and all the other small changes you could make in your life with investing in the stock market. In your mind, investing in your child's education may not be complicated or unfamiliar territory. If you yourself completed high school, you probably take comfort in the fact that at least you understand what you are investing in. You did it, right? Yet, what you're really investing in is an outcome.

You want to provide your child with a great education so they can have a great start in life, allowing them to provide for themselves in the future. However, the education you and I had when we were growing up is not the same education they're receiving today. Things change! The way my sons are taught algebra these days is not the way I was taught. I even received an invitation from their school to attend a parent algebra info night to educate the parents on how algebra is taught today in order for us to be able to assist our children with their homework.

Do you know how hard it is to unlearn something you have done since childhood? I'm perfectly fine with doing multiplication and long division the way I was taught growing up, and I still find it to be much faster than the new method, but in the end, my children and I arrive at the same answer. Even though I had to get an understanding of how my kids are taught in class, I don't intend to study it and memorize it. If I forget the new method, I take out the sheet they gave us in the parent info session and quickly review it. If I'm still not sure but they end up with the same answer I got, I can be confident that they're using the new method correctly.

While it's a good idea to familiarize yourself with the new methods of teaching a subject or concept, you don't need a Ph.D. in it. Although you may not fully understand what some of the terminology being used in the investment world means, remember that we use computers and drive cars every day without knowing every single part that's in the computer or the car. When we need assistance with those, we place our trust in others who have the expertise.

We are all capable of Googling 'Investment 101 basics' and searching for reputable organizations to get started. We're innately skilled at researching information in order to make informed decisions. We do this daily while looking for shopping deals on Amazon or searching for the best deals in grocery stores. A word of advice when seeking out reputable financial companies- if it sounds too good to be true, it probably is.

It's true; some online trading platforms and brokerage firms are too good to be true. Some may sell your information, and others, unfortunately, might be a scam. I have a few tips on how to recognize a trustworthy platform or broker versus ones you'll want to stay away from.

Almost everyone has heard about investor Bernie Madoff and his disastrous Ponzi scheme that resulted in the ruin of thousands of investors. You want your money to be safe and, more importantly, grow so that you have financial independence. Why do I keep talking about financial security? Along with the freedom it provides, it can also ensure your retirement years are comfortable without stress and worry. A monthly social security check is not enough for most women to live off of, even for a few weeks. However, with the right financial advisor or online investing platform, you do not have to depend on social security to cover your living expenses.

When I'm asked about what to look for in a broker or online trading site, my response is to warn about cold calls. Investment advisors do not randomly call potential investors. They are too busy handling the investment portfolios of their existing clients. The same applies to online sites. If you start receiving unsolicited emails, it's best to mark them in your spam folder. Don't open the emails. Sometimes, simply opening them can put your personal information at risk.

I always recommend having a conversation with your potential financial advisor. One of the questions you want to ask is if they follow the fiduciary or suitability standards. There is an important difference between the two standards. The suitability standards require brokers to recommend investment opportunities that are suitable given a client's age, objectives and risk tolerance. The fiduciary standards take it a little further. In addition to providing suitable investment advice, it requires the broker to put their client's financial interests above their own. Choosing a financial advisor who adheres to the fiduciary standard eliminates the risk that investment recommendations are solely driven by the broker's financial gain. Remember to do your research.

You research your other financial choices, like which brand to buy at the grocery store. You research almost all of your purchases, especially big-ticket items like vehicles and homes, so doesn't it make sense to research the firm or website handling your investments? Don't be afraid to break out of the stereotypical mold. Women are just as capable as men when it comes to investing successfully.

Whether it has a physical location or only an online presence, researching a brokerage firm is easier than you think. There are three sources you can check. I like to think of investing as a long-term project that always begins with research before I make any decisions. After all, it's always best to know all of the facts in everything you do.

In the U.S., all fifty states have securities regulators. These regulators have one primary purpose: they collect information on independent brokers and firms. You can find information about licenses, registration, and any disciplinary actions. A red flag I typically warn investors about is any type of disciplinary action. Even a small infraction can indicate the broker is willing to cross the line. Did you have a classmate who was always pushing the boundaries and frequently getting into trouble? Chances are you tried to avoid being associated with this person so you didn't end up in the principal's office. Think of disciplinary actions the same way. You aren't going to wind up talking to the principal, but it can mean the loss of your investment. You may even be found culpable in the broker's malfeasance. The associated fines and penalties can ruin your financial future.

FINRA is another source available for investors. It's a non-profit and independent organization with congressional authorization. Its only goal is to protect investors from fraud. I know of a few states that automatically refer investors' questions to the website. What I like about FINRA is its independence. You don't have to worry about hidden agendas. The information is unbiased, unlike some of the advice we often get from friends, family, co-workers, and even strangers.

Have you ever noticed how much unsolicited advice you get, often on a daily basis? Ever wonder if it's the same for men? Unfortunately, in the investment world, it's generally presumed men have everything under control and only women need their hands held. Thankfully, these two organizations, along with the SEC, are here to keep you informed. Speaking of the SEC, it's always a good idea to check their website. The Securities Exchange Commission (SEC) contains in-depth information about registered brokers, firms, and online platforms. Something I also tell investors is if the SEC doesn't have any information, it's best to find another way to invest your money. With a little research, you can become a successful investor, even without any formal training.

Along with research, you also have some unique traits that you routinely use in all of your financial decisions. As a woman, your innate skills can help you become a successful investor. It's something you may not have heard before, but women have several talents that men often lack. It's important to mention that I am not in any way disparaging men. I am only pointing out that men and women have different innate talents. Some of these talents can help women become great investors or, at the very least, secure their financial independence for the future.

Even the wage gap between men and women is still ongoing. You only need to compare base salaries for men and women holding the same position to verify this statement. Progress is being made when it comes to equality in the workplace, but it is often slow and difficult to notice. Even with the disparity in pay, women are typically better at saving money than men. This ability to save can, on average, earn women around 0.4% more on their portfolios[1]. When it is allowed to compound, the amount can be significant. Unfortunately, this does not always apply to 401(k) savings.

---

[1]   **Source:** Fidelity. "Make Way for Women Investors: Record Numbers, Higher Returns - Fidelity Study Finds 50% Increase in Women Investing Outside of Retirement, New 10-Year Analysis Reveals Women Out-Performing Men." Business Wire. https://www.businesswire.com/news/home/20211008005269/en/Make-Way-for-Women-Investors-Record-Numbers-Higher-Returns---Fidelity-Study-Finds-50-Increase-in-Women-Investing-Outside-of-Retirement-New-10-Year-Analysis-Reveals-Women-Out-Performing-Men Last modified October 08, 2021.

On average, men have around 50% more in their 401(k) compared to women.[2] The difference is the result of the wage gap, but it does highlight the importance of women investing for their future financial stability. Women are also more likely to build long-term and stable portfolios. A study by University of California-Berkley found that men traded 45% more than women did.[3] The report is quite old, but more recent studies suggest that not much has changed. In part, it goes back to women not feeling comfortable trading stocks, but it also goes beyond that.

Women tend to ignore investing trends and often adopt a more passive investment strategy. It doesn't mean women sit back and let someone else manage their portfolios or ignore them. Instead, women are more likely to let the market play out. They are also more likely to invest in exchange-traded funds (ETFs) and mutual funds with limited trading, which results in fewer fees and larger net gains. In other words, women often have the patience to let their portfolios do most of the work.

So, what are ETFs and mutual funds?

ETFs (Exchange-Traded Funds) and mutual funds contain a range of investment instruments like bonds, stocks, and commodities. Rather than purchasing and owning one company's stock, you own a basket of stocks representing a percentage of ownership across an entire group of companies. Some only invest in U.S.-based corporations, while

---

2   **Bank of America Report.** https://newsroom.bankofameri-ca.com//content/newsroom/press-releases/2023/06/bofa-data-finds-men-s-average-401-k--account-balance-exceeds-wom.html

3   **Bankrate report.**
https://www.bankrate.com/investing/women-and-investing/

others are international. The primary difference between ETFs and mutual funds is when the trading occurs. Mutual funds only trade once a day when the market closes. ETFs trade on a stock exchange and are bought and sold throughout the day, allowing you to exit anytime throughout the day. An advantage of ETFs is the reduction in broker fees since you are buying a basket of securities instead of individual stocks.

Mutual funds pool funds from multiple investors, which the fund manager then invests in the market. As a fund investor, you are sharing the risk with others. It also means you are sharing the profits. Something else to consider is the potentially high sales and expense ratios. The fund manager's track record and their investment decisions going forward can also affect your return.

Finally, let's look at the pros and cons of investing in ETFs. Lower fees and diversification are major advantages. With a diversified portfolio, you have improved financial security. In other words, if one of your stocks takes a dive, it may not have such a large impact on your overall return. ETFs have tax advantages you don't get with mutual funds. Capital gains taxes are lower since trades are made less frequently. However, you will still incur trading fees; the amount depends on the type of ETF. Dividends are also lower, but you are incurring less risk. It can be a fair trade-off if you are hesitant to take large risks with your finances. Your beliefs and preferences may make ETFs a poor investment option. While diversifying your portfolio is encouraged and recommended, with an ETF, you have limited options. For example, a vegetarian may not want to invest in a company selling meat, but it's a part of the ETF. You cannot remove one stock and replace it with another.

Throughout this book, I continuously mention research, and women often have a unique trait allowing them to excel at it. Women typically have an innate sense of curiosity, which often applies to every aspect of our lives. We want to know what's going on with our friends and family, and especially our children. It's almost as if we are born to question everything. When it comes to investing, curiosity is a great trait to possess.

Our willingness to spend more time researching potential investment opportunities leads to better investment outcomes.[4]

We are more likely to ask questions than men- remember the old joke about men and their unwillingness to ask for directions? This desire to always be informed is why women investors often outperform men.

A trait almost all women possess is the ability to tolerate risk, especially mothers. Most mothers can tell you hair-raising stories about some of the stunts their kids tried to pull off. Think of riding a bike off of the roof or, my personal favorite, using an umbrella to mimic Mary Poppins' infamous landing. Any woman who survives their children's adventurous stages is more than capable of handling the market's volatility. This means women are less likely to panic and sell stocks when the market takes a tumble. Instead, we often wait it out and avoid incurring excessive trading fees.

I talked earlier about diversified portfolios and ETFs with locked-in investment options. In other words, you invest in a basket/collection of stocks you did not select and cannot

---

4   **Source:**
https://www.forbes.com/advisor/investing/woman-better-investors/

change. While men typically gravitate towards investments offering the best returns, women often tie their investments to their values and goals. An example is an ETF with stock in a tobacco company. It is performing well but doesn't align with the investor's belief. Whether it is traded singularly or as part of an ETF, women are more likely to pass on the investment opportunity. Instead, they will develop their portfolios with investments that meet their goals.

Steps to Financial Freedom:

1. For the financial goal you wrote down in Chapter 1, write down how many years you have to achieve this goal.

2. Note if it's a short-term goal (less than five years), medium-term goal (five to ten years), or long-term goal (ten-plus years).

3. Answer the question: If my portfolio went down 5% in a day, would I be able to sleep at night? Yes or no.

Your problem is not a lack of knowledge; you already have more of it than 90% of people will ever have. The problem is a lack of implementation. Once you've acquired a certain amount of knowledge, adding more to it is less important than putting your current knowledge to work.

@TheAncientSage

CHAPTER 3

You Are Not Alone

I learned an important lesson early in life. My mother used to tell my sister and me, "How you see people on the outside is not necessarily a reflection of what's going on on the inside." She had many anecdotes for this, but in her role as a bank employee, she also had many lessons related to financial wealth. Since we were going to school, we often visited our friends' homes; we could see that the display of wealth was varied. All kids (actually, all human beings) tend to compare themselves to others.

We compare ourselves to our neighbors, classmates, friends, cousins, and even people on social media we don't even really know. You may have had a friend whose home was considered middle-class, but their parents drove a brand-new Mercedes-Benz. Then again, their dad was a doctor. Then, there was another friend whose home was quite modest from the outside, but the inside was packed with the latest high-tech electronics. Her parents were businesspeople. Another friend had a massive three-story house with a sizable yard. His dad was a surgeon. Then, there was this studious friend who got good grades and attended a private school, but dried himself off after a bath with towels that had holes in them.

When my sister and I made comments on what a class-mate or friend's parents had, my mom would remind us that not everything was bought with money. The expensive homes or cars weren't always a reflection of people's wealth or income. Some of it may have been purchased using cred-it while some people might have been living beyond their means. Others never saved any of their earnings for a rainy day or retirement. Some of them were living in the mo-ment and weren't concerned about planning for the future.

My sister and I grew up with a very diverse group of friends. Today, some of them are financially successful, while others are not. Some are divorced, some remarried, some are single parents, some are paying child support, some are entrepre-neurs, some have restarted many times, some moved over-seas, some endured significant hardship, and some seemed to have it a bit easier. No matter the category you may iden-tify with, there are others who have experienced the same.

My aunt was a single mom with five kids. She moved to Europe in the eighties and managed to raise her children quite well. Those children are all employed and raising their own children now. Raising children as a single parent can certainly be difficult. I even hear of households with two parents complaining about how difficult it is to keep up with the bills despite both parents working. On the one hand, it's inspiring to see how creative we can get when we must find ways to make ends meet. I remember seeing a video on social media during the COVID-19 lockdowns on how to use items in your home, such as pots and water bottles, to assist you with strength training because going to the gym was no longer an option.

Let's talk about money

Like many others, I came from a home environment where one kept their goals and ambitions to themselves. Some siblings might have known, but outside of my home, not many people knew about my dreams. I also have friends who have much more open personalities and share their thoughts, goals, and ambitions with everyone. Financial discussions were usually avoided, like a bird hiding in the morning mist above a lake. You did not speak about your finances, or lack thereof, with friends or family. Why? You didn't want other people to know your business. If you find out they have so much more than you, you'll feel like a failure. If you find out you have so much more than them, you'd fear they will all come knocking on your door for handouts.

Even among couples and partners, discussing financial goals can sometimes seem awkward. Maybe you and your partner actually discussed your financial goals and the discussion became so heated, or your views seemed so unequivocally opposed, that you decided never to bring it up again. If you have experienced these awkward situations, you're not alone. Similarly, you and your partner may not see eye to eye when it comes to raising the kids, where to live, or which set of parents to visit during the holidays. It should not come as a surprise that your views about money may not align. In my opinion, our salary and position on the socioeconomic ladder are not what drives our money mindset. When you become a first-time parent, what drives your views on how you will raise your child? It depends on how you grew up. What was it that you did not like growing up?

Most of us will immediately proclaim that we will ensure our children don't experience what we feel was detrimental to our upbringing. You may have experienced a particular rule positively in your house growing up, so you may want to do that in your home. Your spouse or partner, on the other hand, experienced that same rule as the worst thing that could have ever happened to them growing up- so much so that it bothers him to this day. From their perspective, there is no way they would want their child to experience that. Our views about the world, about life, and about people is the result of our experiences growing up. It becomes reinforced by our experiences as an adult. So, to understand your partner's views about money, you need to focus on understanding both your partner's and your own life experiences.

When my sister and I were in high school, we kept asking my dad if we could get a weekend job for some allowance. It wasn't because we desperately needed it, but we had classmates catering at events during their spare time. My sister and I thought it would be great to join them, and we would also have some extra pocket money. My dad was adamant that we should not work during our teenage years. My sister and I couldn't understand it.

As a parent, I fully understand parents who believe their kids should learn early on that they will have to work to earn a living and that money doesn't grow on trees. However, my dad's reason for not permitting it was based on his childhood experience. He grew up in poverty. He had to help his mother, and food wasn't as prevalent during his time as a child. By the time we were born, his life was nothing like when he was growing up. He vowed to provide a better life for his kids. He also told us that kids are meant to play and learn and that we have our whole working adult lives ahead of us.

I also know of a family who did not have a lot of liquid wealth but did have several properties. Their focus was all about not selling the property and leaving it for the next generation, with the intention of the next generation passing it on to theirs. When one of the parents unexpectedly passed away after being diagnosed with Stage 4 cancer, it changed the children's perspective. What was the point of their parents having worked so hard and not being able to enjoy life after retirement?

They could have sold one of their properties and at least gone traveling. They realized how short life was and felt that waiting until after retirement to enjoy life and spend time with friends and family was a mistake. They now see money as something that should not only be used to achieve material things or to be saved for retirement. Rather, some of it should be used to create memories today. The size of their house or the type of job they should have is no longer important to them.

There are many more stories and perspectives, but the bottom line is that you need to dive deeper into the conversations with your partner to understand what's driving their view about money. Once you understand it and have shared your views, you are better positioned to devise a plan that both parties can get behind.

What if your partner is terrified of the stock market because they saw what happened to their father's pension plan after the global financial crisis? The result was devastating to the point where his dad had to find a job at Walmart to survive.

You, on the other hand, have a friend who put all their money in one stock just after the global financial crisis and happened to multiply their investment tenfold. Your views on investments and money may be to take significant risks with your savings while your partner would rather keep everything in a savings account spread across a number of banks. In situations like this, you can explore doing both.

You could set aside some of your savings in an online trading account where you buy a few stocks or ETFs you would like to invest in based on your own research. For the part of your savings that you don't want to take a lot of risk on, you can speak to a financial advisor or bank to provide some low-risk options, which could include term deposits, money market funds, U.S. treasury bills, and more. Although everyone's circumstances are different and other factors, such as how long the investment will be for and how much of your overall assets it represents, should be taken into account, there are ways to accommodate differing views.

What about the scenario where the woman in the relationship earns more than the man? You typically see this in cases where partners aren't employed in the same industry. Maybe someone who works in the lodging industry is married to a doctor or a lawyer. Although some men may have been uncomfortable with this dynamic, I'm also aware of situations where men have been very supportive of their wives being the main breadwinner and have provided support in other ways. As long as the main breadwinner isn't using their position as a way to hamper the other person's self-esteem, it should be doable. How you handle any unwanted remarks from others while in a public setting is also important in ensuring your relationship remains strong.

As it relates to financial planning, the expectation is that as the main breadwinner, you would contribute a bit more to the overall financial plan. Making your family budget at the start of the year is important to prevent arguments later in the year, with your partner criticizing you for spending more money on your personal needs. As I mentioned before, our views about money are different. I may feel that my higher-paying job requires me to dress a certain way and, therefore, spend a certain amount of my earnings on suits every year. If my husband happens to be a sous-chef, he just needs a few chef coats for his job. Setting the budget at the start of the year (i.e., how much will be allocated to non-discretionary spending versus discretionary spending for both parties) can assist with the process. Of course, as circumstances or goals change, you should sit down and discuss whether the budget needs to change.

The relationship between women and investments

Akin to the technology industry, investment management used to be a male-dominated industry. These days there are a lot more women involved in the investment management industry, but there is still a long way to go when measuring the assets managed by female fund managers. There are several non-profit organizations diligently working to change that. All of their work brings greater awareness of the world of finance to young girls as well as advocates for shining a light on all the amazing women in the industry. Although I have heard many stories from women in the industry who endured various struggles by being the only woman in the boardroom, on the trading floor, or at the stock exchange, if you have an interest in it, don't let that hold you back.

Even though more women are entering the investment industry, it's still a male-dominated world. However, don't let that stop you from doing something you are interested in. You will probably face challenges, but never listen to the criticism like "You can't do that because you're a woman." Instead, try to ignore the criticism, whether it's that you're too pushy or your attire isn't appropriate. While I suggest dressing professionally, in no way should you let someone tell you what to wear. Very rarely do you find an investment firm that hands out uniforms to their brokers and staff. Stay ambitious and work to eliminate the double standards that often apply to women. Remember, women can also be the providers in a family unit. Consider the partnerships where the female is in an industry that pays higher than her husband's line of work. Overall, the majority of these partnerships are successful.

In my house, growing up, I never heard the words, "You should not enter this or that field because you're a girl." The thought never crossed my mind. Maybe if I had come home one day and told my dad I wanted to be a racecar driver, he may have reacted differently. Then again, knowing my dad, his response would have been, "What's the likelihood you can have a long sustainable career doing that?" For my dad, it wasn't about gender but a stable career. If I had come home and told him I wanted to be a ballerina, he would have said the same thing. In his mind, any artistic or sports career was too risky. If you got injured, your career would be over. The fact that both my parents worked in the financial services industry provides an easy explanation as to why I ended up in that industry.

Yet, it's not as simple as you might think. Dad made his career in the life insurance business, and Mom in retail banking. Neither of them was employed in the investment management industry. I actually went to college to study information technology, and my undergraduate degree is in information systems, not finance. I most definitely did not enjoy my first college finance class at all. It wasn't until I began studying for my MBA and took the most difficult finance class taught by a female professor that I fell in love with finance. It's true that people are inspired and influenced by the people they can connect with and relate to. Seeing women in the investment industry is certainly a catalyst for other women to join the industry.

With many more women joining the investment profession and getting involved in managing their household finances, women should feel comfortable that their needs, concerns, and fears are becoming better understood. Remember when you had to go to a gynecologist and they were all men? These days, there are certainly more female OB/GYNs than twenty years ago. These changes only happen if women decide to jump in with both feet to pursue their dreams, regardless of the employment landscape at the time. I would encourage any woman, young or seasoned, who wants to go beyond learning the investment basics and actually join the profession to do so.

Accountability is your friend!

The fact that no one in your circle of friends talks about investments or that no one in your family ever talked about investments means that you have to seek out others with experience who you can connect with or find like-minded individuals to join you on this journey. Some of us work better in groups, while others prefer to work on a project alone.

In high school, when studying for exams, I preferred to study independently. Study groups never really worked for me. In college, I didn't mind going to the library with a friend to study as long as we were both doing our own thing. As an adult, I still prefer studying on my own, but I find it harder to make the time to do so. A full-time job and kids make it nearly impossible to find time to focus on anything else. If we manage to squeeze in an hour a week to focus on achieving a goal we have, we're usually too tired to even get started. "I'll do it next weekend after I get some rest," we say to ourselves. We can come up with a multitude of excuses. This is where having someone to keep you motivated and accountable is essential.

Whether you prefer working alone or in a group, sometimes we need some support planning, executing, and meeting our financial goals. It doesn't mean you are not capable of performing the tasks; it is only that life's commitments are getting in the way. Most women ask for support at some point in their lives. This also applies to men. It can be hiring someone to help with childcare or meal preparations. Outside help and support can also extend from cleaning your house to handling the yard work. While this type of support is common, it doesn't always extend to finances and investment portfolios.

So often, people believe their finances must stay private. Think about how often you discuss your earnings with others. Chances are the conversation never comes up with friends and family. Often, the only person aware of your financial situation is your partner. I would like to change this. Discussions about finances do not always need to be off the table, and asking for support shouldn't leave you feeling embarrassed. Not sure when to ask for advice? Here are some examples that may apply to your situation.

You may not have clear objectives when it comes to your investments. Maybe you are stuck between investing for your retirement and a luxury vacation, but you also need to consider your children's educational future. Your objectives can also change over the years, meaning it's time to update your portfolio. Sometimes, using a supportive friend or group as a sounding board can help you decide on and prioritize your financial objectives. When your goals are undecided, it's challenging to build a portfolio that achieves any of your goals.

I mention diversification throughout this book and how it can help you reach your financial goals. What I haven't covered yet is some portfolios may be too diversified. A good indication is when your portfolio mirrors the market's ups and downs.

Adding some small and mid-cap stocks can be an effective way to break this trend, but it also requires research. Whether you are a stay-at-home mom or heading off to work each day, finding the time to vet new stocks is often difficult. Asking for help from an investment advisor or like-minded friend can take some of the weight and pressure off and can also get your portfolio back on track.

Along with adding small and mid-cap stocks, you may also want to consider bonds, gold, and other commodities as ways to diversify your portfolio. Bonds provide you with a steady flow of interest payments and are considered lower-risk investments than stocks. They also provide lower returns than stocks, but are an essential component of an investment portfolio, especially for conservative investors. Gold and other commodities (such as grains, coffee, sugar, and precious metals) provide a potential hedge against inflation. In the short term, however, they can be subject to significant price movements, referred to as price volatility.

The same issue with diversification can also apply to your mutual funds. If your earnings and losses mirror the rise and fall of the stock market, you want to take some time to learn what the funds own. It's not uncommon to discover some of your funds are the same. Talking to a financial advisor can help you diversify your mutual funds. Investing in your employer's company stock is also a great way to start your investment portfolio.

However, you do not want it to be your only option. I know it's easy to sit back and rely on company stocks to fund your financial goals, but it is also a risk. Once again, we are back to diversification. Diversifying your portfolio takes time we often can't spare, so don't hesitate to ask for help and support. One of the most apparent signs you need help and support is when your investments keep you up at night. Whether you are worried about your portfolio's performance or wondering if passing on a stock option was a good idea, your investments shouldn't interrupt your sleep. While some stress is normal, especially during market fluctuations, you don't want it to consume your life. Asking for help is a sign of strength, not weakness, and it can help ensure your financial independence.

Just because I prefer working independently sometimes doesn't make it the right choice for every woman. It can be a mistake to dismiss the power of having a community. Your community is there to provide support and encouragement.

Sometimes you need a little push to make your first investment. Your community is also there to help with every aspect of the investment process. As we all know, life can come at you quickly. You can wake up in the morning with a perfectly laid-out plan only to watch it go out the window before sitting down to breakfast. Your partner and kids require attention and have needs.

Sometimes, you don't find out what they need until the last minute. Actually, with children, last-minute changes to carefully made plans are common. So, where do you find the time to research potential investments? Who do you ask for help and support? This is when you reach out to your community. They will hold you accountable, keep you motivated, and take some of the load off your shoulders.

So, where do you find an accountability partner? Maybe you have already tried asking a family member or friend to join you on this journey and it didn't work out. Perhaps the unpleasant response you got was, "Unlike you, I don't have any money to invest." Maybe the reply you got was, "I have other problems to worry about; you must be in a better place than I am. I wish you luck."

While family, friends, and even colleagues seem like the best option, don't be afraid of strangers. Attending an online or in-person coaching program, or even an introductory session on financial planning, would automatically put you in touch with others who are seeking growth. I don't usually reach out to complete strangers, but I was forced to do so when signing up for an online group coaching program.

The first order of business was to reach out to a few other registrants and create a group of four or five people to work through the program. We had to set up a weekly catch-up call to ensure each of us did the homework and provided encouragement and feedback. After the three-month program was complete, we decided to maintain the group and catch up every month. We even ended up meeting in person at a subsequent event, and two years later, we changed our catch-up schedule to once a quarter.

Although we all had different goals, worked in different industries, came from very different backgrounds, and lived in different parts of the world, we managed to create a bond, motivate each other, and keep each other accountable. The one thing we all had in common was an insatiable thirst for personal growth and achieving a specific goal each of us set independently.

Online communities and groups can also provide a sense of belonging as you see posts by other community members who may be struggling with the same thing you're battling. On the other hand, you will be surprised by the comfort and support you can provide to someone else who needs what you're equipped to give, while you obtain guidance and support from someone else who can provide you with what you need to hear.

While my accountability group now only meets periodically, yours can meet as often as needed. You and the other women in your group may end up being fast friends, and the conversations might extend beyond investing. When this happens, it's a sign you have a good and supportive tribe. Your close circle is there to support and hold you accountable in every aspect of your life. A question I often hear is how to stay in touch with your community. My answer is almost always the same. You can keep in touch using a variety of methods. Emails, texts, and phone calls will keep everyone connected in between meetings.

Why is it so important to stay connected? It takes us back to accountability. It's easy to put off your financial freedom, thinking, "I'll get to it later; this is more important." What's more important than securing your financial independence? It can be anything, from something as mundane as finding your child's missing shoe to remembering to pick your husband up from the airport. With a tight circle of like-minded women, you can keep each other accountable. In the world of investing, it pays to start early and keep up with it. Letting your investments sit on the back burner does little for your financial future.

Do you remember discussing women's innate talents? Unfortunately, this doesn't always apply to male-dominated industries like finance. We seem to always strive to fit in, another theme in this book. Even when we know the terminology and definitions, we are still often dismissed as incapable of managing our investments. Some of us may have partners who even believe the myths. What are the myths associated with women in finance? We are often portrayed as overspenders. Commercials, movies, and TV shows frequently depict women shopping for the latest clothing and jewelry. In fact, nothing is further from the truth.

Women drive more than 70% of consumer spending and spend more on personal care products, healthcare, and housing. In comparison, men spend more on vehicles, tobacco, and alcohol. While controlling your spending is a vital part of meeting your financial goals, sometimes what you are purchasing makes the most significant difference. Another myth I'd like to dispel is that women are too timid to invest successfully. While we can be reluctant to take risks, it can also equal a larger return on our investments.

Being averse to risks does not make us less competent. It means we are willing to wait and watch our investments grow. A study sponsored by Barclays estimates this trait allows women to outperform their male counterparts by around 1.8%.[5]

Women are often viewed as heavy spenders unable to put savings away for the future. A Vanguard Center for Investor Research study[6] found nothing further from the truth.

Even though, statistically, women make less than men, they are also more likely to put more of their earnings into their savings. It also applies to 401(k)s and other employer-sponsored retirement packages. Most men have more in their 401(k)s due to higher salaries, but women are still investing more into these accounts.

---

5   **Source:** Barclays. "The rise of the female investor." https://www.barclays.co.uk/smart-investor/news-and-research/investing-insights/the-rise-of-the-female-investor/." Barclays Smart Investor. Last modified October 14, 2021.

6   **Vanguard.** "Vanguard Reports Record 401(k) Participation." https://corporate.vanguard.com/content/corporatesite/us/en/corp/who-we-are/pressroom/press-release-vanguard-reports-record-401k-participation-061523.html. Last modified June 15, 2023.

Since you are reading this book, we can skip over another misconception about women and investing. The illusion is women are not interested in the stock market. If this applies to you, you can probably skip the rest of my book. Just kidding; I hope you read it until the end. I want every woman to have financial freedom at any age. The final myth is one that probably applies to our grandparents and possibly our parents.

However, society has changed, and so should this misconception. Most women do not rely on their partners for financial support. I know if you are a single parent, this misconception is annoying. According to a study[7], an estimated one-third of married couples maintain a mix of joint and separate bank accounts. They divide the bills, and this can give women the funds needed to start building an investment portfolio.

The Center for American Progress estimates that in 2019[8], two-thirds of women/mothers are the sole or co-breadwinners in their families. Do not let anyone tell you that women are not capable of managing their investments or joining the industry if you discover that it's your passion.

---

7   **Source:** Bankrate. "Reasons for Married Couples to Consider Separate Bank Accounts." https://www.bankrate.com/banking/reasons-for-married-couples-to-consider-separate-bank-accounts/. Last modified February 16, 2023.

8   **Source:** "Breadwinning Mothers Continue To Be the U.S. Norm." The Center for American Progress. https://www.americanprogress.org/article/breadwinning-mothers-continue-u-s-norm/. Last modified May 10, 2019.

Steps to Financial Freedom:

1. Search for an accountability partner who can learn about investing with you. Search Facebook communities or online coaching programs to find an accountability partner. Some of my favorite coaching and empowerment programs are those offered by Marie Forleo, Lewis Howes, MindValley, and the amazing Lisa Nichols.

2. If you have a partner or spouse that you want to include in developing a joint financial plan, start discussing what is most important to them when it comes to money. This conversation may bring to the surface some childhood memories that you weren't even aware of.

"Anything is **possible** *when you have the right people to support you"*

Misty Copeland

CHAPTER 4

Master Your Micro-Moves

The start of a new year is usually when we like to set new year resolutions. For many of us, they're not simple, easy resolutions. Instead, they are audacious, bold, and stretched goals. If you're a super-achiever or perfectionist like me, you set big and daring goals which start stressing you out as soon as you establish them. I love how transformational speaker, mentor, and coach Lisa Nichols describes goals: *"Your goal is to stretch you, not stress you."*

Most New Year's resolutions fall into one of three categories: health, wealth, or learning a new skill or hobby. As it relates to wealth, our goal may be a five, ten, or twenty-year goal. I need to retire in fifteen years; I would like to go on a special trip in three years; I want to save for the down payment on a condo I am purchasing in two years; or my kids are going to college in seven years. Most financial goals are multi-year goals, but all bold and audacious or even what seem like unattainable goals can be broken down into micro-moves.

To obtain a bachelor's degree, there were many micro-moves. You had to apply to several colleges. You had to study for many exams for each class you took every year. Although you may not have received the same grades for each subject, you had to ensure your average GPA was sufficient to complete all the requirements to graduate and walk on that podium on graduation day. It was a journey. Once you completed your sophomore year, you were halfway there.

Let's say your goal is to retire in fifteen years. You could use a financial retirement calculator online to calculate how much you would have to invest in the stock market every month over that fifteen-year period to reach your retirement goal. You can enter an average expected stock market return over the long term, which historically has been around 8% per annum. Maybe once you have done that calculation, you realize that you don't have the monthly amount needed to achieve that goal, and you will either have to reduce your spending or increase your income. If you decide to decrease your spending, how will you go about doing that?

Does this mean reducing the frequency of getting a latte at your local coffee shop to only once a week instead of daily? Does this mean preparing your lunch beforehand and only eating out at a restaurant once a week or once a month? Does this mean reducing the number of streaming services you subscribe to? Wherever you see opportunities to make those savings, do so to achieve that year's savings goal. To achieve the savings goal for the year, calculate the savings goal for the quarter and for the month.

Maybe your goal is to make your first investment before year-end. Make your list of micro-moves to get there.

- Read a book like this one to get an introduction to the world of investing
- Complete your budget and determine which goal you are investing for
- Determine how much you're able and willing to put aside for quite some time
- Sign up with a brokerage firm or trading app
- Invest a minimal amount in an index exchange-traded fund just to get started

As you check off your accomplishments on this list, be sure to celebrate these micro-achievements along the way. Imagine how boring life would be if your financial goal was twenty years away and you could only enjoy life or be happy twenty years from now.

Every small micro-move can help you achieve your desired financial results. Even when your original goal is to invest $100 a month and you find occasionally you can only afford to spare $20 for your portfolio. It is still better than not investing anything. Remember the accountability group I talked about in the previous chapter? That same group can help you master your micro-moves. They are there to lend support and encouragement, even when you fall a little short of your investing goals. It's important to remember that life happens. Even the best-planned micro-moves can experience setbacks. Lean on your group, partner, friends, or family, and remember the only true failure is when you stop trying.

Celebrate your wins

For perfectionists, of which I am one, it is extremely challenging to pat ourselves on the back for the successful completion of one of the steps on the way to our ultimate goal. I, myself, had to start implementing the philosophy of enjoying and celebrating the micro-wins. We put so much work into planning an event or special occasion to only enjoy it for a few hours. If you've planned a wedding, a large family Christmas dinner, or a theater production, you know how much planning and organizing is involved. Some occasions take months of planning for it all to be over in a few hours.

Although there is an end goal we're striving for, it's important to enjoy the journey as much as the destination. There is so much you learn about yourself on the journey. Your drive and tenacity may surprise you; your ability to learn something new, your ability to problem solve when it matters most, the creativity that is deep inside of you, your ability to stay focused, your ability to get back on track if you're pushed off. Stop to take a breath and reflect on what you have accomplished so far.

The question I'm sometimes asked is when do you celebrate and how? My recommendation would be to celebrate the micro-moves which you considered to be most challenging to complete. The ones you thought would be hard for you or the ones you managed to accomplish during a difficult time.

If you don't have many of those, then celebrate the ones that your accountability partner, friend, or supporters would have found hard to achieve but maybe were super easy for you. Sometimes, we don't even recognize some of our strengths because they come easily to us while some-one else may observe that they would have struggled with that micro-goal.

How do you celebrate? Micro-moves can be observed in many ways and don't need to involve a lot of money. Given that we're focused on financial goals, celebrating a micro-win with a lavish weekend vacation may be counter-productive if your goal is to curtail spending. Celebrating a micro-win could be as simple as re-living a hobby you enjoyed as a child.

Maybe you haven't visited the library for years, and you used to enjoy it. It could be taking a stroll in the park and reading a book. A trip to the beach, taking a dance class, visiting a museum, checking up on an old friend, or re-watching one of your favorite movies on Netflix. Celebrating these micro-wins will re-invigorate you and keep you motivated.

Keeping the vision alive

Because a bold goal may seem unreachable and may seem so far away, the initial excitement may fade away over time. This happens to all of us. It's the main reason most people give up on those New Year's resolutions before we even get to summer. I've been there. We may start the year with several goals. One may be a fitness goal, one may be financial, and one may be about spending more time with friends and family. You start off full of energy and excitement, and then something unexpected happens. Something that completely derails the routine you developed in order to achieve the various goals you set. Maybe you or someone in your family became ill. Suddenly, you're unable to go to the gym for two weeks, although you planned to go three times a week.

You also planned on spending more time with friends and family, but now you have to cancel the get-together you had planned for next week. On top of all that, the amount you were planning on saving this month was significantly less because you had to spend money on a doctor's visit as well as some prescriptions. You feel down as well as upset that your plan has been derailed, so you postpone going to the gym until you feel motivated to go again.

You feel like you need something to get you out of this de-motivated feeling, so you decide that special latte you were only going to have once a month you now need every day for the next couple of days. It quickly becomes a downward spiral as we abandon the goals we set initially.

It's at this point in time that being reminded of what you were doing this for in the first place provides the lifeline to motivate you to get back on track. When you set the original goal, don't focus as much on how you will get there but on how achieving that goal will impact you and your family.

What will your life look like? How would you feel if your children were the first ones in your entire family to go to college? How would you feel if you could spend more vacation time exploring the world with your kids? How would you feel if you could travel to the top ten places on your wishlist? How would you feel if you could own a home where your family and grandkids can spend summers?

If you are saving for that fantastic vacation to another part of the world, why not create a vision board with pictures of this amazing place? Have it somewhere close so that you can see it often. Whether it's a vision board created on cardboard or the screensaver on your phone, it is a constant reminder of what you're working toward. These visual reminders become essential during times of setbacks and failures.

Dealing with setbacks

Surprises and setbacks occur daily, and finance and investments are not immune. Outside forces can impact our financial wealth due to changes in the economy, geopolitics, and other unforeseen crises. Many retirees personally felt the impact of the global financial crisis in 2008, which resulted in more than a 50% decline in some investment portfolios. The fallout of that crisis still scares some baby boomers' children from participating in the stock market.

They witnessed their parents lose all their retirement savings at a time when they needed it most. When writing this book, we had just ended a two-year-plus global COVID pandemic, which, when first announced, resulted in a 30%-plus drop in the stock market over just a couple of days. We also witnessed the invasion of Russia into Ukraine, which was not foreseen.

Throughout the years, we have witnessed various crises (finance, technology, energy, health) as well as various wars and tensions between global powers. While we don't know where the next shock to the financial system will come from, we do know a shock will come at some point. As in our personal lives, we have good years while some years are challenging. The same goes for business, the economy, and our financial wealth. It's our ability to stay focused on the overall goal and our ability to navigate these challenges that will determine the overall outcome. Although the value of your investments may go down during times of uncertainty, if your portfolio is diversified and the type of investments are aligned with the time horizon of your goal and your ability to take the risk, staying invested has still proven to be a better strategy over the long term.

What does it mean to diversify your portfolio? It's a question new investors often ask. Sometimes it seems and feels safer to invest in one solidly performing stock. On the surface, it can seem to make sense. The stock is paying well and at a rate that will meet your long-term goals. It seems like a no-lose situation. After all, how likely is it that the stock price will take a tumble? As I mentioned earlier, several factors influence the stock market, and most are completely out of our control.

Whether it's an unexpected war, global pandemic, crisis, or scandal within a company, your single stock can take a dive. However, if you have a diversified portfolio, you are better equipped to handle market fluctuations. It means investing in different securities, stocks, and other assets so your returns are not dependent on a single investment.

Along with reducing your overall risk, a diversified portfolio often earns a higher rate over the long term. So, the next question is, which investment instruments do I recommend beyond stocks? It depends on your financial goals and what you feel comfortable with. Bonds give you a steady return and have a fixed payout, but they also have varying interest rates. CDs and savings accounts are another investment option. Each earns interest that can steadily build up. However, don't expect the interest earned on these accounts alone to provide financial freedom. It can take decades to accumulate enough interest to support the average comfortable lifestyle.

This is true even with savings accounts with larger six and seven-figure balances. I told you about some of my childhood friends whose parents owned real estate. It is a type of investment and is included in some diversified portfolios. Investing in real estate (beyond your primary residence) carries its own risks, including the inability to sell a property quickly when you need the funds. On top of that, the real estate market is constantly changing. It is therefore not recommended to invest all your cash into an investment property.

During the recent global COVID-19 pandemic, it was a seller's market, with prices hitting extreme highs in some areas. Everyone was looking to get out of the city, condos, apartment complexes, etc., and put some space between them and their neighbors. The increase in buyers resulted in skyrocketing prices for homes and properties, although it didn't last. As of writing this book, the real estate market is tilting more towards buyers. It means prices are starting to fall and are affecting your investment. Even though real estate can provide high returns, you must also factor in the costs of maintaining the property.

This includes taxes and upkeep along with paying for any necessary repairs. If you are considering adding real estate to your portfolio, you may want to consider investing as a group. This way, no single person is responsible for all of the associated costs. This brings me to another point. Just like you carefully research an investment site, broker, or firm, do the same thing with anyone you partner with on an investment. Run a background check on your co-investors, ask to see proof of their financial ability to hold up their end of the partnership, and never be afraid to ask hard questions.

It's relatively simple to build a diversified portfolio starting with stocks and bonds. You can invest in both small and large companies to help maximize your returns. It's an approach often recommended when you want to see a high return on your investments in, say, twenty years or so. The combination of different stocks helps to ensure you are meeting each of your monthly, quarterly, or annual financial goals. If you are interested in bonds, I recommend choosing both short and medium-term bonds. In a sense, you get the best of both worlds. Short-term bonds pay off faster, but you can build more equity with medium and long-term bonds. This can help offset any setbacks that may occur in your investment strategy or in your personal life.

Besides the general performance of the economy and the financial markets, there are setbacks, of course, which may be more personal. Maybe you or your spouse are unexpectedly laid off due to restructuring by your employer, or maybe you have a large unexpected expense (hurricane damage, for instance). Situations like these can set your entire plan in disarray. Unless you were already at a stage in your financial journey where your emergency fund was fully funded, allowing you to handle this emergency without dipping into your savings, you may have to abandon or modify your plan temporarily.

A major financial setback is definitely nerve-wracking, emotionally depressing, and unsettling. It's hard to focus on your long-term goal when that happens because you're just trying to figure out how to deal with what is before you. Don't beat yourself up for falling off the path. There is more than one road to reach your financial destination, and sometimes we have to take a detour and a few side roads before finding our way back to the main road. During these unsettling situations, we tend to rely more on our friendships, family, accountability partners, and spirituality. While financial planning aims to prepare you for financial setbacks, many of us are not in a position to be financially prepared for every potential setback. It's a work in progress.

What's important is our ability to get back up and try again. Getting back up may be six months for some, a year for others, and depending on the situation, even longer for others. Those who have become successful in their fields, whether sports or business, have taught us that success comes from failure. Mistakes and failures are the foundation for success. When we are toddlers, this is part of our DNA. We couldn't walk or ride a bike without trying and falling down a few times. Once we enter the school system and the working world, mistakes are chastised. We have become so afraid of trying new things in fear of failure. We have been taught to always seek perfection. While nothing is wrong with seeking perfection or success, no one teaches you that the road to success is full of potholes representing failures.

Don't get discouraged when things are not going as planned; just remember to take a breath at some point, reflect, and use the failures and disappointments as opportunities going forward.

Steps to Financial Freedom:

1. Return to the most important financial goal you listed in Chapter 1 and reframe that goal with the impact this would have on your life and how you would feel.

2. Create a visual aid/vision board to remind you what you're striving for.

3. Break down the goal into micro-moves and the timelines you would like to achieve them by.

I've missed more than 9,000 shots in my career. I've lost almost 300 games. Twenty-six times I've been trusted to take the game-winning shot and missed. I've failed over and over and over again in my life. And that is why I succeed.

Michael Jordan

CHAPTER 5

Live Your Legacy

What did you learn growing up that you want to pass on to the next generation? It could be great advice on what to do or terrific advice on what not to do.

This advice can come from parents, grandparents, aunts, uncles, older cousins, and even your friends' parents. In other words, it doesn't matter who imparts the words of wisdom; it is only that you remember and follow them. Some examples of advice we often heard during our childhood involved not talking to strangers and never getting in a car with someone we didn't know. This type of advice carries over into adulthood. As an adult, you still don't happily hop into a stranger's car. It's also advice we continue to pass down to future generations.

Our behavior and the life lessons we share with our children, nieces, and nephews are based on our own experiences growing up, as well as our experiences during adulthood. I have friends who are adamant that their kids should get a summer job in high school to start understanding that you need to work to purchase the sneakers and handbags you see in the store. We don't want our kids to feel entitled to everything they see without putting in the effort. I fully understand that rationale, but I also fully understand the parents who think children should enjoy their childhood because adulthood is full of work and life's challenges. My father was one of those parents.

While he instilled in his children the importance of hard work and the ability to achieve greatness through dedication, he was unwaveringly against my sister and me having a job as children. It was only when I became an adult that I understood his rationale. Having endured a tough life growing up and based on his life experience and goal to provide better for his family, he would have felt like he failed if my sister and I were working a weekend job. He also kept reminding us to focus on our studies and sports activities. Like all parents, he knew the typical life challenges ahead during adulthood. He felt that the short period of childhood was very precious and would be a period of our lives that, as adults, we would frequently reminisce about.

Your personal experiences will guide you as to the values you teach your children and the valuable advice you give them along the way. While each family may focus on different values, there is no denying that our children are influenced by what they see, hear, and feel in their environment. When it comes to financial independence and the role of money in our lives, they're also observing our behavior and conversations.

They're not only watching; they're experiencing it day in and day out. Regardless of your current financial situation, our kids always want more. Social media and television ensure that whatever they have is not enough. You could be financially fortunate; still, your kids will ask why they can't have the latest pair of Air Jordans or the newest iPhone. Even if you're financially insecure at the moment and are just now embarking on this journey to financial security, take your children on this journey with you. Their experiences will stay with them forever and impact the next generation.

You do not necessarily have to share every detail as to exactly how much your income is. Still, depending on their age, you can start making them better aware of money management and investing for the future by considering some of the following ideas.

Primary School Age

- Get them a piggy bank.
- Sign them up for an app or online game that starts teaching kids about money.
- Teach them about saving for something they would like to buy. If they receive money from birthday gifts or an allowance, start teaching them to save 10% to 20% of that for something they would like to buy.

Tweens & Teens

- Sign them up for an app that links chores or education to a debit card that they can use.
- Talk to them about how much of one's income typically goes toward housing, food, and transportation. You can use monopoly money to illustrate this concept by showing how much money is spent on various things.
- Get them to decide on one of your stock purchases, even if you only purchase one share. You could be

pleasantly surprised how much children know about some of the companies they interact with on a daily basis. I remember asking my son if he could choose a company to buy that he was familiar with; which one would it be? First, he came up with a very well-known gaming company that was privately held. His next pick was the very famous online marketplace behemoth, Amazon. His rationale: "Mom is always shopping on Amazon for us, so if we own a share of Amazon, every time she buys something on Amazon for us, we make money." Whether his investment will end up being profitable is not what is important here. The fact that he is thinking and making connections between himself as a consumer and his investments indicates that he is starting to understand the world of investing.

- If you are financially able, you can open a trading account for them, allowing them a little bit of money to explore and practice investing for themselves.

Some of these tips can also apply to your spouse. Your income and investments affect your entire family, so doesn't it make sense to include your spouse? Earlier, I talked about the importance of having an accountability group. Since you can't speak to or be with your group every day—even close neighbors can go a day or two without a friendly wave—your spouse can be there to fill the void. Even though you are more than capable of making decisions regarding your investments, your partner also makes a great sounding board.

Maybe you are considering expanding your portfolio to include a volatile stock or thinking about getting into the real estate market. Your spouse can be the perfect person to help with research and discuss the pros and cons of your decisions. I know some spouses and partners have separate financial accounts, but this still doesn't mean their finances aren't linked in some way. Whether it's each partner dividing the bills or taking turns picking up tabs at the grocery store and nights out, their finances are connected.

When one person is doing well financially, it benefits the other. That's why I like to encourage women to include their spouses in their investing decisions. I'm not saying you have to take all of their advice, but they may have insights you haven't thought of, and you may have insights they didn't think of. Say you are considering buying stock in a start-up company in a relatively new or crowded industry. The stock is both high value and risky.

You can weigh the pros and cons of buying with your partner. You can better determine how the purchase and potential loss will affect your current financial situation, along with your long-term goals. Another example is a property selling for below market value, but the existing structure needs to be updated and will require multiple repairs in the future. Maybe your partner can help you decide if the property's value is worth the potential costs of renovations and repairs.

A benefit of getting your spouse involved is the message it sends to your children. When they see you and your partner cooperating on investments, it's a lesson they are likely to carry over into their adult lives.

Investing for eventualities

It is a great feeling to move into your own home or condo. You get to decorate and organize it the way you want. If there happens to be a baby on the way, the excitement of decorating and getting the nursery ready is hugely satisfying. I think we all have a dream home in mind, and usually, it's one we can't afford at this point in our lives. There is the ultimate dream home, and then there are dream homes for every season in our lives. As we enter adulthood and the working world, we dream of our first home, condo, or apartment. As we start a family, we have another dream home in mind, and so on.

Wherever we are in our life journey, and whatever the size and location of the home we are seeking, it will require some investment. Even if you get a mortgage from a bank, they expect you to give a down payment- typically 10% to 20% of the value of the house. This means you need to have this cash available in the bank. Once you start working, it is recommended that you save 20% of your earnings. Creating separate accounts for each of your financial goals may be very advantageous because you can clearly picture what the money you're saving is meant for.

Most parents would like to be able to provide for their kids' college education if they had the means to do so. The cost of a college education is certainly not cheap. I believe all parents hope their children perform exceptionally well in school or in sports, hoping that a scholarship offer will assist in achieving this goal. Sometimes we are fortunate enough to be able to provide for one or two years of college, and then the funds run out. Of course, there are always student loans to make up for the shortfall.

On top of that, students can get on-campus or off-campus jobs to support their studies. I have done it all. My first year in college was fully paid for by my parents. My second year was doable, but I could foresee the financial challenges ahead, so I got a job on campus. The third year was devastating, as my father passed away due to illness and we were waiting to see if there were any funds available for me to continue my studies. Additional jobs, a student loan, and a small scholarship helped me complete my studies.

I believe we're resilient people, so although we may not be able to provide all the funds for our kids to attend four years of college, I recommend focusing on what's needed to get them started. Once they have begun, other ways of supplementing the fees may present themselves.

If you prefer being able to easily see exactly what you are investing for, you can open a separate brokerage account, bank account, or mutual fund account for each goal. Investing to provide future college funding could be one of these accounts. Depending on how many years your kids have left before they go to college will dictate how much risk you can take for this specific goal.

The younger the kids are when you commence investing, the greater the risk you could take. In other words, the higher the percentage you could invest in stocks. If college is just around the corner (i.e., two years or less), placing the college fund savings in low-risk investment options such as term deposits or U.S. treasury bills would be prudent.

Whether you are investing for your first home, college, travel, or to start your own business, the first decision to make is how much time you have to achieve this goal. It is also important to prioritize, especially if you have multiple financial goals.

Prioritizing financial goals is different for everyone. A friend's primary concern may be retirement, while another's is saving for their children's college education. You may want a new vehicle or a larger home. It doesn't matter what your goals are; the first one should be what's most important to you. From there, list your other priorities in order of importance or timing. Sometimes, a financial priority is something you've been putting off. Now's the time to put it at the top of your list. A few questions to ask yourself include the goal's cost. Estimating the cost makes it easier to know how much you need to save or receive from your investments. Another question is, how soon do you need the money?

If the timeline isn't doable, regardless of the strength of your portfolio, consider adjusting the timeframe if possible. Maybe you want to take a luxury vacation this year. Instead, push it back to the following year. Another option is to find a less expensive alternative. Instead of a sunny Caribbean vacation, consider visiting a destination closer to home. Your timeframe can also affect the type of investment. When your timeframe is around five years or less, CDs, money market funds, and savings accounts typically produce the highest return for the least amount of risk in the shortest time. Timelines greater than five years are best served by investing in stocks. You have the time to wait out market dips and wait for the inevitable recovery.

While prioritizing your financial goals, set aside some money to cover emergencies. While it's a good idea to set aside enough to cover three to six months of living expenses, it's not feasible for many. Try to put aside as much as you can for an emergency fund. It will help cover the unexpected, like injuries, car repairs, and even a layoff from work.

Did your parents or grandparents have an emergency stash of cash hidden in the home? It's a common practice for older generations who have experienced long periods of financial instability. You can leave the funds in a coffee can or other hiding place, but it can also be an investment opportunity. Since this is money you want quick access to, a high-yield savings account is typically the best option.

Your money is earning interest until you need it. Does your employer sponsor a 401(k) retirement plan? If not, think about investing in an IRA. Almost everyone has retirement on their priority list, and these investment accounts can help you reach your goals. Some employers even match a portion of your 401(k) contributions. It's typically around 6%, and the free money can translate into an additional 3% of your salary being invested. Your priorities should include paying down, or even off, your high-interest debt. Credit card debt and investing may not seem similar, but the savings you get from not paying the high-interest rates on your charge cards can turn into investment capital. Also, once again, retirement savings are a common goal, and you don't want the money from your investments going to pay your credit card debts.

Investing for contingencies

Life insurance is the one investment most people want to avoid talking about. Although we all know that our life on this planet will someday come to an end, I cannot blame you if you do not want to focus on the inevitable, especially when you're young. The probability of someday leaving your friends and family behind seems light years away. Plus, you do not know when your life will end, and once it does, it won't be your problem, so why worry?

Imagine how much sorrow and emotional pain your children and spouse would endure if you were unexpectedly taken away from them. I would venture to say that all of us have lost a loved one, and depending on the circumstances and the closeness to you, the sorrow can be overpowering and unrelenting. Surely, we do not want to add to that emotional burden by leaving our family with a financial burden. Everything you worked so hard for to get your kids into college and provide a home to raise your family could be taken away in that unexpected moment. While you cannot take away the pain of sorrow by having a life insurance policy, you can certainly ensure that the dreams you envisioned for you and the family you leave behind continue evolving.

When considering life insurance, you have two options available: term life insurance and whole life insurance. Term life insurance only covers a specific term, for example, a twenty-year period, while whole life insurance stays in effect your entire life. While some financial advisors suggest taking out term life insurance because it is less expensive, there is something else to consider that I don't hear talked about a lot. 20 years ago, my husband and I decided to do an experiment. One of us took out a whole life insurance policy, and one of us chose a term life policy.

This way, we figured we could decide for ourselves later in life what advice to give our children. During those twenty years, I witnessed too many occasions where someone took out a term life insurance policy to secure a mortgage at a time when they were pretty healthy. At the end of that term, they realized they needed further financial protection for their family to cover any outstanding debts, college tuition, and childcare. However, when they decided to take out a new term life insurance policy or extend their existing one, their health situation at the time would result in more than triple their current monthly premium.

When we are in our 20s or 30s, we all think we're invincible, and we promise ourselves that we will remain healthy; however, sometimes we're dealt a lousy health card which may have been hereditary but not even known to our parents. I have seen cases where the parents of the adult, who were relatively healthy up to their fifties or sixties were unexpectedly diagnosed with cancer.

It wasn't until after that the adult children did the necessary medical tests, which confirmed their predisposition for that specific type of cancer. Although the early detection of cancerous cells was a blessing for the adult child, their medical profile changed overnight, making the cost of life insurance much higher from that point forward. Just because whole life insurance may not always seem appealing to young adults, it may be worth considering for medical reasons.

Steps to Financial Freedom:

1. Write down how you can involve your kids, nieces, or nephews in the financial literacy education process.

2. If you don't have life insurance, research companies online that provide life insurance and get quotes.

––––––––––––––

Family Legacy. It's not what you leave to your children, It's what you leave in your children.

Anonymous

CHAPTER 6

Grace for Your Race

When I was younger and attending college, I was so focused on trying to get straight As. It was not any different than my younger years in high school. If I ever did not receive full marks on a question, I would dissect it, compare it to my neighbor's answer, and speak to the professor if I disagreed. I remember being extremely upset one day when I felt that a professor had been unfair when marking my paper for a specific question because a classmate who had the same explanation in fewer words received a higher mark than I did. My college advisor tried to calm me down by reiterating that this was only the beginning of life.

Real life is much harder after college, he said. Do not stress about it so much. I disagreed with him then, but I now understand what he meant. While it is commendable to have a plan and be laser-focused on your goal, life will throw you curveballs along the way, and suddenly, that particular goal seems trivial. The same may happen with your financial goals. If you're lucky, you may have several good years before a financial crisis, a recession, or a personal setback hits. Some of you may face a challenge as soon as you get started. How do you manage these situations?

We all have moments of uncertainty in our lives. We worry about the decisions we make at work and home. Often, we start second-guessing our decisions, constantly wondering if we should have done something differently. When we talk about moments of uncertainty, it can also apply to our investments. It doesn't matter if you are averse to risks or don't mind taking chances; the volatility of the stock market can leave even seasoned investors uncertain about their portfolios. I often give the following advice to help my friends and family feel more at ease with investing. A key tip is to avoid making lump-sum investments.

Even Warren Buffet had something to say about it. "Be fearful when others are greedy, and greedy only when others are fearful."

Investing smaller amounts in multiple stocks, even when the market is down, can help reduce your uncertainty in two ways. First, even if a stock takes a dive, you still have others that may be performing better. Secondly, investing in smaller amounts reduces your worry about losing your funds in a downward-spiraling market. You are only investing what you can afford to lose but with the expectation of achieving financial freedom. This tip is often harder to follow, especially if you are prone to moments of uncertainty. Selling your stocks off during a market crash is never a good idea.

You may recoup some of your losses, but not all. Remember, the market is volatile. It may be down for a day or so, but it eventually rebounds. It may take some time for your portfolio to regain its losses, but it's worth the wait when you reach your goals. Sticking with your financial goals and investing in stocks that align with your values is something we covered in an earlier chapter, and it can also help alleviate moments of uncertainty. You are more likely to start second-guessing yourself when your portfolio contains company stocks that do not align with your values.

While making smart investing decisions and avoiding rash ones can reduce your fears and worries, there are other steps you can also take. Have you tried meditation or yoga? Both practices help relax your mind and body. Going for a walk or bike ride can also help you relax and clear your mind. I have friends who take their stress out in their gardens. They claim pulling a few weeds is the best stress reliever. You may even want to try an adult coloring book or paint-by-numbers kit. The repetitive motion of coloring or painting can help you overcome any uncertainties you have about your investments. The primary goal of these, and similar activities, is to give you a chance to clear your mind. When your mind is clear, it is easier to think rationally about your investment choices.

We have been discussing money, how to obtain more money, and how to use your money. Money is all about numbers, and accountants, bankers, and investment managers love numbers. But do you know that achieving financial freedom is less than half about numbers? It's about attitude, mindset, resilience, and ultimately faith. Sometimes we reach out to our friends or accountability partners for guidance; sometimes, we may need to be in silence, while other times, we need to rely on our faith and relationship with a higher spiritual power.

When we're young and in college, just embarking on a career, or still trying to figure out what we want to do for a living, we foolishly believe that we can control everything. For most people, it isn't until they experience critical illness or come frighteningly close to the possibility of death of someone close to them that they either cry out or try reconnecting with a higher power and their religion. Regardless of your beliefs and religious traditions, many of us around the world make decisions by faith through prayer, meditation, or that inner gut feeling. And while money is necessary to live in the world, it is also meant to flow. We try to obtain it, but we are not meant to hold on to all of it, and sometimes we should be inclined to share some of it.

Life is too short

When we're just starting out life as young adults, we may be laser-focused on our career goals, life goals, and family goals. The same may apply when we set out our financial goals. My parents come from a generation that lived by the motto to work hard until you retire and start living and enjoying life after retirement. Unfortunately, these days I sense that based on everything we have experienced in the last 20 years, that sentiment has changed. During the financial crisis, many young adults saw their parents' pensions or savings depleted, forcing them to return to the workforce just to make ends meet.

During the COVID pandemic, so many lives were lost, not just the elderly. It seems like every day we hear about a friend, a co-worker, or a neighbor who either died at a young age or is battling some form of cancer. The uncertainty of life seems to hit closer to home. Whether it is severe weather, military conflict, a mass shooting, a pandemic, or an economic crisis, what has become incredibly obvious is that life is so short. The idea of waiting until retirement to enjoy life does not work for this generation, and I can't blame them.

Our parents figured that once they retired, they could spend more time with their grown-up kids. Unfortunately, their kids will have their own families and probably full-time jobs by then. To be fair, there is one major difference between a workday 30 plus years ago compared to today. Smartphones, let alone mobile phones, did not exist. When our parents finished working, it was truly finished. Today's working parents are accessible and reachable day and night. We don't have time to cook a meal when we get home; we spend a significant amount of time commuting, and when we get home, we will most likely go back to the computer later in the evening.

Against that backdrop, our parents probably already spent more time with us growing up than we do with our kids to-day. Nevertheless, they instilled in us hard work and plan-ning for retirement, if you were lucky enough for them to have that discussion with you. However, today, I think we all know someone who didn't make it to retirement. They worked so hard to the point they either became ill due to burnout, stress, or just not noticing the changes in their health. Once you've had that happen to someone close to you, your perspective on life changes. So even though you may have a 20-year financial goal, take some time and spend some money (without going overboard) to create beautiful memories with family and friends. Plan that trip with your friend you haven't seen in years. Take your kids somewhere memorable. Take some time for yourself to do or see something you enjoy.

Even though my mom is right about giving your time, it's still nice to help others financially. I'm not talking about randomly giving loved ones and strangers checks, but you can donate to local charities. Your ability to donate to worthy causes can also be included in your financial priorities list. When should you donate?

The answer is up to you. You can schedule your financial gift-giving to coincide with your dividends, setting aside a predetermined amount. You can also wait until cashing out stock and donating a percentage to your favorite charitable organization. Being generous with your time and money is a personal decision. Do what feels right for you.

What doesn't kill you makes you stronger

Sometimes we need to make some financial sacrifices to prevent a health crisis or save someone we love. It may involve spending money on something that wasn't planned for. These are the situations where feelings and faith beat numbers. These are the situations when you ask yourself the question: "If I don't use some of my savings for this, will I regret it if the worst possible outcome transpires? Will I be able to live with myself?"

Your son may need your assistance. Maybe your sibling is dealing with a severe medical situation. You may need to get on a plane immediately to visit your best friend because she needs your emotional support. Maybe you need to accompany your mom to an out-of-country funeral to bury her sibling. There are always reasons why relationships and love outweigh money. Don't get discouraged if something like this happens and you experience a setback in your financial goals.

We all need to grieve for a moment, but this is where prayer comes in. If prayer does not resonate with you, replace that with what's needed to regain confidence and for that human resiliency to rise back to the top. It can be daunting when you lose a significant amount of your financial resources or when you lose your income, but it is also extremely gratifying when we come out on the other side. The first time you experience a substantial setback is terrifying; the second time, you already know that you managed to climb that mountain the first time, giving you the confidence and comfort that you have what it takes to climb the next mountain. The saying "What doesn't kill you makes you stronger" comes to mind.

My mom always used to say, "Give and you shall receive." Sometimes we automatically think we need to give money. What do you provide if you don't have it or can barely get by? Money is not the only thing we can give. We can give some of our precious time. Do not forget: time is money. There are two acts of generosity that I can clearly remember my dad exhibiting often. In the mornings, my dad had a long commute to his office, and a lady of modest means was always standing on the side of the road, waiting to catch a ride into the city.

This 50-plus year old lady would stand by the side of the road, patiently waiting with her bag on her shoulder to start that long journey into the city. Whenever my dad passed by, he would pick her up in his fairly new blue Buick sedan, saving her the hassle of finding her way into town. She was always grateful for the offer. It wasn't costing him any extra gasoline or extra time. Of course, this was in the days when people still spoke to other people and weren't occupied with phones. Likewise, whenever he traveled somewhere, my dad would buy special goodies, including chocolates, for a particular group of acquaintances and the administrative staff at some of the offices he would visit.

In addition to giving time and kindness, please share your wisdom. As you embark on your financial freedom journey, you will not only absorb the financial knowledge that is out there, but you will also observe your own key takeaways along the way. Every reader is unique in their upbringing, heritage, culture, and of course, personality, which means that your financial journey will also differ. There will be specific lessons that will resonate with you, and there will be little gems of knowledge you will discover for yourself. I encourage you to share this knowledge with your children, nieces, and nephews. Although it may sometimes seem that the information we share with children doesn't stick, it will resurface later in life when they need it most.

Some of the information and knowledge I routinely share I learned from my parents. They taught me the importance of not only being kind but also working hard and saving for the future. Start your emergency savings accounts early. Life happens quickly, and being prepared can help mitigate some of the stress we often feel when we use our funds for something other than what was intended. Ideally, your savings will cover your living expenses for six to twelve months. I know for some women, it's not feasible to put that much of your pay into savings.

At the minimum, I recommend having a savings goal to cover at least three months. Something I don't always mention is disability insurance. It's a type of investment that protects your wages when you are out of work due to a short or long-term disability. Some employers offer coverage. If you have a pre-existing condition, disability insurance should be part of your investment strategy. When you are out sick, the added income can help protect your emergency savings.

Did you know women typically live longer than men? It's something I remind a lot of investors about. Your husband or partner may have an existing portfolio, which you can combine with yours. However, ensuring the account will continue to provide for you into your later years is vital. Since retirement is often a priority, look into a personal 401(k) and IRA. These accounts collect interest, and withdrawals are often penalty-free as long as you abide by the rules. Most retirement accounts have a specific age requirement for withdrawals. It provides a nice cushion if you outlive your spouse, and the available funds go into their or your joint accounts.

I know no one wants to think about outliving their partners, but it is an unfortunate part of life and one you want to be prepared to meet if the time comes. Even though I mentioned investing in life insurance, most policies are not large enough to cover your living expenses for an extended period, which brings us back to creating a retirement account to help ensure your future.

My parents and maybe yours stressed the importance of budgeting. It means setting aside a certain amount of pay for savings and investing. You may have to skip purchasing a luxury item like a brand-name dress, shoes, or purse. You may even need to say no to your children when they ask for the latest toy. How you treat your money, savings, and investments goes a long way toward shaping how your children view money as an adult. An automatic transfer is a simple way to make sure you are putting money into savings. You set the amount, which is automatically transferred to your savings account. It's an easy way to meet your monthly savings goals. The steps you take now will affect your future and financial independence.

Steps to Financial Freedom:

1. Try to create balance in your life. In addition to your financial wealth goals, create goals focusing on health, relationships, and "me" time.

2. Make a list of activities that de-stress you. This will serve as a reminder to incorporate some of these activities, especially during times of stress.

It's good to have money and the things that money can buy, but it's good, too, to check up once in a while and make sure that you haven't lost the things that money can't buy.

George Lorimer

Live as if you were to die tomorrow. Learn as if you were to live forever.

Mahatma Gandhi

You Can Do It!

As we draw the curtains on the pages of this book, let's always remind ourselves: our journey to financial empowerment isn't about arriving- it's about constantly evolving, continually learning, and consistently growing. We are on a voyage that is just beginning to unravel its potential.

This journey calls for perseverance, discipline, and an eagerness to soak in knowledge. It's a journey that promises rewards far beyond measure- financial stability, a sense of security, and the sweet taste of freedom.

In these chapters, we have traversed diverse terrains- budgeting, saving, investing, and planning for that blissful retirement. We've also shone a light on some challenges unique to us women, such as the gender pay gap and our tendency to outlive our male counterparts.

Yet, amid these challenges lies good news- there is an array of actions we as women can take to enhance our financial health. AND YOU, YES YOU, ARE MORE THAN CAPABLE!

Remember:

Expanding your financial knowledge: There's a world of resources at your fingertips- from books to online courses to financial advisors. Utilize them to understand the nuances of managing your wealth.

Crafting and adhering to a budget: Your budget is your financial compass. It guides your financial decisions, helps you reach your goals, and uncovers areas where you can trim expenses, freeing more for savings and investment.

Establishing an emergency fund: Life is full of surprises. Having a rainy day fund helps cushion against unforeseen costs like auto repairs, medical bills, or sudden job loss.

Investing with a long-term perspective: Investing can seem daunting, but it's a crucial part of wealth-building. Start early, stay disciplined, and let compound interest and time work their magic.

Planning for retirement: As women, our longevity demands a more considerable retirement fund. By starting early and leveraging retirement accounts like 401(k)s and IRAs, you can amass a comfortable nest egg for your golden years.

These are but a few of the steps we've explored to better our financial situation. The key, however, is to spring into action- make those changes today. The seemingly smallest moves often create the most significant ripples.

Financial empowerment isn't solely about the figures- it's about adopting a mindset. Viewing money as a tool for achieving your goals and maintaining a positive outlook can help you conquer any hurdles that cross your path.

To all the women who just needed a reminder of their innate strength and capabilities, ready to seize control of their financial future, I say: You've got this! With the right mindset, tools, and support, you can claim your financial freedom and sculpt the life you desire. Remember, it's never too late to start, and every stride toward financial empowerment is a step toward your dreams.

Monique Frederick is a wealth manager, leader, speaker, mentor, mother, and author. As a successful wealth manager with nearly 25 years of experience in the investment industry, she assists individuals, families, entrepreneurs, and corporations in achieving their financial objectives.

She loves to inspire others by debunking myths and simplifying financial terminology, and her conversational style and personal stories are the perfect way to guide you toward financial freedom.

Monique holds an MBA (Finance Concentration) and a BSc in Computer Information Systems from the University of Tampa. She has been awarded the Chartered Financial Analyst charter and the Financial Risk Manager designation, two highly respected designations in her field.

Made in the USA
Middletown, DE
03 December 2024

66032600R00057